Date of Ret

Illustrated
DUCATI & CAGIVA
BUYER'S GUIDE™

Mick Walker

Aston Publications

Sole distributors for the USA

Motorbooks International
Publishers & Wholesalers Inc.
Osceola, Wisconsin 54020, USA

Published in 1989 by Aston Publications Limited
Bourne End House, Harvest Hill, Bourne End
Bucks. SL8 5JJ

ISBN 0 946627 35 5

Printed in Great Britain by The Amadeus Press Ltd
Huddersfield West Yorkshire

Sole distributors to the UK book trade
Springfield Books Ltd
Norman Road
Denby Dale
Huddersfield
West Yorkshire HD8 8TH

Sole distributors for the USA
Motorbooks International
Osceola
Wisconsin 54020
United States

Acknowledgements

Way back in 1961 I bought a brand new Ducati 250 Daytona (Diana outside Britain). This machine, one of the very first of its type imported, started a love affair between these unique sporting motorcycles from Bologna, Italy, and myself which has lasted over a quarter of a century.

Not that I have exclusively ridden or owned Ducatis since then. In fact it has been my good fortune to get to ride an amazing array of two-wheelers from humble mopeds through to such exotica as MV Agusta and Bimota superbikes.

Even so, Ducati has played a prominent role in my motorcycling career – having commuted, raced, tuned, been a dealer, parts distributor and importer, even sponsored other riders on them – and now writing about them!

However, this wide experience has, I hope, not created a rose-tinted complex. Ducatis, like virtually any motorcycle, are not without their faults. In fact, as I'm sure most enthusiasts for the marque will agree, a Ducati is made up of either brilliantly good or downright bad – with very little centre ground. This in turn can both impress and infuriate, often at the same time. But nonetheless this Jekyll and Hyde personality gives these bikes true character with a capital C.

Because of this owners will usually put up with faults which on another machine would convince them to trade it in for something else. In other words there's something about a Ducati which makes its owner far more loyal than he should be!

I therefore dedicate this book to all Ducati enthusiasts around the world – I have discovered over the years that the vast majority are truly the salt of the earth.

In compiling this Buyer's Guide I have included Cagiva, because not only do they now own Ducati, but since June 1983 the two marques have been joined together commercially for, I am sure, the benefit of both companies and customers alike.

Although Cagiva is a much younger company than Ducati its progress since its inception in September 1978 has been nothing short of amazing. As the company's first British importer I have been fortunate enough to watch its progress, often from behind the scenes, from Day One.

Both factories have assisted me with photographs, as have many Ducati and Cagiva enthusiasts, including – in no particular order – Nigel Ball, Gerolamo Bettoni, Brian Davis, Mike Clay, Jim Curry, Ken Kavanagh, Alan Kirk, Eric Green, Stuart Mather, John Powell, Andrew Reynolds, Philip Tooth, Paul Weston, Martin Heather, Ron Titenor and Don Upshaw.

A special thanks to Denise Preston of the Italian Trade Centre, London for organising both photographs and visits to Italy.

If I have forgotten anyone I can but apologize, it was not my intention.

The rest of the photographs came from my own collection, which has been built up over many years.

My thanks also go to my secretary, Carol Green, for typing the manuscript.

Finally, to Anthony Pritchard of Aston Publications for approaching me with the original idea.

I hope the result makes interesting reading and at the same time will assist owners and potential owners alike in answering some of the many questions which usually remain hidden from general view.

I'm sure if you get half as much fun and enjoyment from being involved with Ducati or Cagiva as I have, you'll be happy.

Mick Walker
Wisbech, Cambridgeshire
January 1989

3

How To Use This Book

This is not intended to be yet another book on the history of motorcycling, or one of particular technical details, rather it is to help the owner, restorer, potential buyer or simply a committed enthusiast for either Ducati or Cagiva motorcycles to avoid a few of the pitfalls which might catch out the unwary. But most of all the intention is to provide a general guide on just what bikes are the most sought after – collectable – of the many models produced by the two Italian concerns since their respective entries into the motorcycle field.

Like the stock market, collecting, restoring or just using a motorcycle can go up or down in value and nobody, myself included, has all the answers. So you should become involved with Ducati or Cagiva through genuine enthusiasm not simply as a financial investment for the future!

Prices
To simplify matters all prices quoted are approximate. For readers with different currencies a simple conversion will reveal the value. However, with currency fluctuations this can only be a rough guide and should *not* be taken as the exact price. In any case prices are constantly changing, so the best system is to study the various national and local press publications before starting your search.

Rating system

★ A model which has not received particular attention or enthusiasm from potential owners in the past. Usually readily available – whether produced originally in small or large numbers.

May have potential in the future, and has the advantage of the lowest current price. Conversely the majority of machines in this category will remain largely unwanted.

★ ★ In this category come the motorcycles which proved popular when new, are still in widespread use and *may* in future, when fewer are around, appreciate in buyer/collector interest and therefore value. But you are taking

a risk as an investment.

★ ★ ★ This is the average, one which should hold its value, but you are never going to make a fortune out of it. Offers its owner considerable enjoyment out on the open road. Buy for use rather than investment.

★ ★ ★ ★ Valuable now – and in the future. But because of its desirability will already be expensive. It will continue to rise in future, but just how much is uncertain.

★ ★ ★ ★ ★ The real classic. If you find one at a realistic price snap it up now, it's going to become a special bike that even more people will want in the future, meaning that its value will go up faster than machines in the other star ratings.

Important note
Prices are *greatly* influenced by condition, serviceability and originality – but no guide can make up for the experienced eye, so if you do not feel you come into this category make sure you find someone who does and take him along before parting with your money. Work needed to be done, including parts, should be deducted from estimated values.

However much you may feel you need the bike, it is best to be patient. By adopting this method you are less likely to suffer heartache.

I have attempted, by writing this book, to help Ducati/Cagiva buyers find a good bike at a fair price. Over the years I have found the vast majority of Ducati/Cagiva owners to be the salt of the earth, and they are very likely to share a mutual respect and sincere interest in the product. But don't accept that this will be the case every time. Size up each seller independently. It is better to be safe than sorry!

Finally specials, whether home built, or professionally constructed, are generally of considerably less value than (original) standard production models of the same vintage. This is because they reflect one man's dream, rather than a concept which will appeal to a wider audience.

Contents

Chapter 1

Setting the Scene

Today, the name Ducati stirs the same levels of passion in motorcycling circles as do the words Ferrari or Porsche with the four-wheel fraternity. With a host of fanatical enthusiasts for the famous Italian marque all over the world – but in particular, Germany, Japan, the United States, Australia and Britain – one would have thought that Ducati Meccanica Spa would have been a commercially successful and stable company. Far from it, the last decade has seen the company go from crisis to crisis, until in 1985 they were officially absorbed into the Cagiva Group – who had only commenced two-wheel activities as late as September 1978. How a company with so much less history was able to achieve this is recounted in the section dealing with Cagiva later in the book.

The Ducati factory complex was, and still is, based at Borgo Panigale on the northern outskirts of Bologna. Pre-war it had produced photographic and electrical equipment. Postwar the electrical side was continued after motorcycle manufacture had started but in the mid-1950s the motorcycling and electrical sides of the business went their independent ways, even though to this day they occupy sites next to each other.

Like Innocenti and Piaggio, famous for their Lambretta and Vespa scooters, Ducati was one of the big Italian engineering concerns that had to transfer to new peace-time products at the end of the war. But whereas the other two industrial giants concentrated their two-wheel efforts on a complete machine, Ducati – through Aldo Farinelli – created the Cucciolo (Little Pup), an auxiliary 49 cc four-stroke engine unit, which was designed expressly to fit ordinary pedal cycles and help Italians return to personal transport at the cheapest possible price.

Huge numbers of this micro-engine were produced in the ten-year period from when production got under way in 1946, and the success of this venture was to pave the way for Ducati's entry into the world of small motorcycles of 60, 65, 98 and 124 cc capacity. But unlike the Cucciolo, which had unfamiliar pull-rods for operating the tiny valves, these ohv newcomers had the conventional pushrod operation.

Although Ducati continued to expand – and took an interest in motorcycle sport through long-distance trials and record breaking, it was not until the arrival in May 1954 of Ing. Fabio Taglioni that the Ducati legend really began.

Taglioni – or "Dr T" as he is known to countless Ducati buffs around the world – was a designer of great talent, a racing enthusiast whose other interests of photography and flowers have also brought him considerable recognition.

Taglioni had begun his engineering career whilst studying at Bologna University in the late 1940s, and before joining Ducati he had been with FB Mondial, at that time together with MV Agusta, the most significant name in the lightweight categories of Grand Prix racing. But it was only after Taglioni had joined Ducati that he was given the opportunity to display his full range of skills.

His first design for his new employers was the 100 Gran Sport. This was to prove an outstanding design – not only for what it achieved during its own lifetime but because it formed the basis for the majority of the company's programme of both production roadsters and racers for many years afterwards, and clearly pointed the way ahead into the 1960s and beyond.

Two other men who were to play vital roles in how the motorcycle side of Ducati progressed in its formative years, up to 1965, were Dr Giuseppe Montano, the managing director, and Dr Cosimo Calcagnile, the company's general secretary. Ultimately Montano was to retire at the end of the 1960s, when the company was at a low ebb and in deep financial trouble, but Calcagnile was still part of the scene until the early 1980s, although effectively stripped of much of his earlier power.

The other dominating themes throughout the company's history were to be the financial and commercial decisions at boardroom level. These displayed a marked contrast to the reliability and consistency of Ing. Taglioni's

design genius, as will become crystal clear over the succeeding pages.

The reason why this early history has been examined is because without understanding just how much influence Taglioni's designs had – and how these were tampered with, after 1965, by the financial restraints of successive managements – the reader would not be able to understand why certain models appeared and why others did not.

It is also important for the reader to realize that the word Ducati has not always added up to something which spells the magic it does today. As recently as 1971-72 many owners in Britain, for example, were dissatisfied because the official importer was not keen on supplying spares to owners who had purchased a Ducati from another importer – Vic Camp and Bill Hannah, respectively. This whole sorry saga is outside the scope of this particular book, but still needs a mention to highlight just how quickly the legend has been cemented since then.

Another factor has been the rapid rise in prices of new Ducatis. Although never really cheap, the advent of the larger-capacity V-twin models in the early 1970s brought one significant increase and this was followed in the 1980s by Ducati producing solely large-capacity models which are near the very top of the world's market place for two-wheelers –

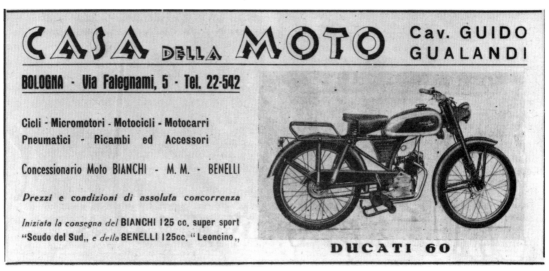

1951 advertisement for Ducati's first motorcycle, the ohv 60; the author has an example in his collection.

"Doctor T" – Ing. Fabio Taglioni, chief designer at Ducati for three decades, with one of his creations, a Mike Hailwood Replica V-twin.

right up there with companies such as BMW and Harley-Davidson. Because of this prices of older models, including the singles, have risen sharply in the last five years. The high current new price structure has further helped the older bike market because it has encouraged investment in restoration. Because large numbers of singles and earlier V-twins were made, this has meant that buyers have a wider choice than they would have for several other prestige marques, such as MV Agusta or Laverda, for example.

Although new Ducatis are very expensive and the price of a restored older example has shot up rapidly, because of the large number manufactured in the past, it is still possible to find a bargain – or something for almost nothing which needs a lot of time and work spent on it. These cheaper machines mean that an enthusiastic *talented* amateur mechanic without much money can still own a Ducati. Thus the current ownership of the marque spans all facets of the financial divide – and long may it remain so. To me it will be a sad day indeed when the only Ducati owners are those with enough money to be able to *afford* one regardless of price.

Allied to the growth of the Ducati legend has been the owners' clubs around the world (described in detail in Chapter 21). The main attraction of belonging to an owners' club is that it puts you in touch with others of a like mind and enthusiasm.

Another reason for Ducatis being viewed in a totally different light from any other motorcycle has been the rapid growth in the number of books on the subject. In 1980 not one single title had appeared exclusively on the subject (except maintenence books such as workshop manuals); today there are several. Luckily for owners and potential buyers this literature has broadened the amount of information to a point where the quality of Ducati's engineering has been matched by the high level of research which has taken place. A further reason for Ducatis being popular is that, unlike certain other marques, they can be rebuilt: generally spare parts are still available (the latter does not apply to the early pushrods and Cucciolo!).

8

Chapter 2

Push-rods and Pull-rods

★ ★ ★ ★	98 Super Sport 1954-55
★ ★ ★	98 Sport 1953-58
★	Others 1946-66

History

Ducati began much the same as many other names in the automotive world by selling basic transport, rather than prestigious sportsters. In fact, in Ducati's case this was a humble "clip-on" engine assembly rather than a complete machine. Called the Cucciolo (Little Pup), this was a best-seller which not only provided affordable transport for Italy's masses in the early post-war days but in addition earned the capital needed for further expansion. The Cucciolo first appeared at the end of 1945.

From this micro-motor came a whole line of small-capacity mopeds and motorcycles which, until the mid-1950s, were the company's main source of revenue, the first being the Ducati 60 of 1950. This was quickly followed by a whole succession of engine capacities, including 65, 85, 98 and 124 cc.

Cucciolo

The original Cucciolo stemmed from one man, Aldo Farinelli. He had begun work on the innovative design in 1942, during the Second World War, and because of this production was able to commence much quicker than would have otherwise been possible. In addition, Farinelli's design was a four-stroke, which gave it a distinct advantage over the two-stroke opposition soon to appear headed by the Mosquito from Garelli.

Its' valve operation was effected by *pull*-rods rather than *push*-rods and was built in unit with a two-speed pre-selector gearbox and nine-plate all-metal clutch running in oil. All shafts ran on rollers, including the camshaft and those in the gearbox.

The engine unit, together with exhaust and fuel tank, was supplied in a kit by Ducati, both for customers to fit on to their existing pedal cycle and to companies such as Britax in England, who began importing the Cucciolo in 1949 and later offered a complete machine. But in those early days (up to 1950) Ducati was purely an engine supplier.

Riding a Cucciolo-engined cycle was hardly more difficult than a conventional pedal cycle. The gears were pre-selected by positioning the bicycle pedals. To pre-select low gear the left pedal had to be moved forward; the clutch lever on the handlebar was then operated and the gear engaged. To change to top gear the right pedal was placed forward to pre-select and the clutch lever was operated again. The normal starting procedure was to pedal off in neutral, operate the exhaust valve lifter, engage bottom gear, release the exhaust valve and open the throttle. That simple!

After a period of free-wheeling with the engine ticking over or stationary, it was important that the throttle was opened gently to avoid snatch in the transmission when the drive was taken up. It was also important to maintain the bottom bracket bearings in perfect adjustment, otherwise the gear-change could become difficult. An internally toothed gear wheel was the link between the pedals and the engine.

When it first went on sale in Britain in late 1949 the Cucciolo cost £40, almost twice as much as the other half-dozen or so "motor attachments" as they were then known. However, even then Ducati's engineering standards were praised, with *Motor Cycling* describing the Cucciolo as: "Beautifully engineered." Later models, post-1955, had fully enclosed valve gear – see below.

Amazingly the Cucciolo engine served not only as an everyday workhorse but also powered several road racers (Britax marketed a dustbin-faired Cucciolo-powered machine) – and even gained world speed records for its class!

What to look for
Considering the vast numbers of Cucciolos constructed (over 400,000) very few survive to-

day. However, it is still possible to find one at an autojumble or elsewhere. The biggest problem is spares – there are virtually no dealers with any stocks. So make sure everything is there before buying one. For a genuine restoration you will also need a period cycle (should you only find the engine unit).

Star rating: One star
A difficult one this. Its main interest must lie in the fact that it is the first of the family, even though it could hardly be further from one of the V-twin super sportsters of the late 1980s. The same applies to either the later M55 engine (with enclosed valve gear), 55 R moped with rigid frame or 55 E deluxe moped with spring frame.

60 and 65 cc motorcycles
These were manufactured between 1950 and 1958, and were not imported by Britax during their reign as British concessionaires (1949-56), although the company which superseded them, S.D. Sullam (1956-58), brought in a few of the 65 T and 65 TL models during 1956 and 1957.

The 48 cc Cucciolo micro-engine, Ducati's first venture into the two-wheel world, made its début in the late 1940s.

British importer's advertisement proclaiming the virtues of Cucciolo power.

10

What to look for

My advice is don't bother unless the machine is complete and running, as spares will be impossible to find, although some little known old-established dealer in Italy may have some stashed away under his counter!

Star rating: One star

Hardly worth the effort.

98 cc motorcycle

There were four models of the push-rod 98 cc motorcycle: 98 TL, 98 T, 98 N and 98 Sport. N and T were base models with spartan specifications. The base model was the N with 5.5 bhp, three gears and single seat. The T featured more power, 6 bhp, four gears and a dual-seat. The TL had the same mechanics, but higher bars, separate pillion seat and crashbars.

The one to aim for is the Sport which had 6.8 bhp, four gears, drop bars, flyscreen (on later models only) and a much more sporting

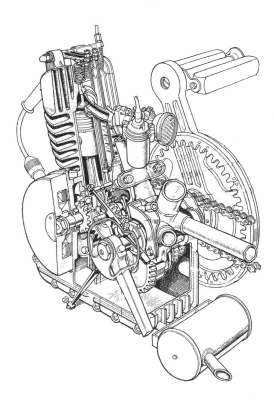

The Cucciolo engine assembly.

appearance. But the biggest difference was an oil-cooler, which was in a deeply finned compartment at the front of the wet-sump crankcase.

Motor Cycling, in their 22 November, 1957 issue, said the 98 Sport was: "A connoisseur's machine in the Ultra-Light Category," and "Expensive – but exclusive." They rounded their test up with: "One point is extremely unusual – in fact, almost unique – everyone who rode the machine fell in love with it!"

A very limited number of the even higher-tuned 98 Super Sport models were constructed for the long-distance road races in Italy. These can be distinguished by their larger SS/22 racing carb (standard MA 20 B), clip-on bars, megaphone exhaust and rear set footrests – and, of course, special bits such as cam and piston within the engine. All the 98 cc models shared an open beam-type frame.

What to look for

Like all the pre-ohc models, the 98s are today a rare sight – and suffer a mutual spares problem.

Star rating: 98 T, N and TL, One Star; 98 Sport, Three Stars; 98 Super Sport, Four Stars

If you find an original 98 Sport grab it, if you uncover a similar condition 98 Super Sport steal it! The cooking models are much less attractive and therefore far less valuable.

125 T and TV

The largest of the Ducati push-rod line – excluding, of course the *Il Muletto* (The Mule) *Motocarro* (three-wheel goods truck), which had a 199 cc engine size.

The 125 TV first appeared at the end of 1957, and although the engine unit was clearly based on the 98 cc push-rod unit it was considerably different in appearance, with a much sturdier and heavier frame (duplex, with twin front downtubes), uprated suspension, full-width alloy hubs, dual-seat and larger fuel tank. But the most notable difference was the Triumph-like headlamp nacelle. The 125 T was essentially the same machine, but without the headlamp nacelle.

By 1959 only the T remained, and this was discontinued the following year. A sports version was never offered, as by this time produc-

The 65T motorcycle, 1953-58. The engine was based on the Cucciolo unit.

The 98 Sport: the dropped bars, flyscreen and sleek lines appealed to Italian youth.

tion of the ohc models was in full swing and the push-rod models were instantly obsolete.

What to look for

As with the 60 and 65 models, the 125 push-rods don't have much going for them today, except to say just how much motorcycling – and Ducati themselves – developed. Usual problem with spares and for that matter information too.

Star rating: One star
No hopers, even for the most enthusiastic Ducati nut.

85 N, T, Sport and Bronco
The first 85, the N, appeared late in 1958. A strange mishmash from Ducati parts bins. Frame from 125 TV, forks from 98 S and engine unit based on three-speed 65 unit! Hardly a potion to set the motorcycling scene alight. The 85 T came in 1959 and this had a new tank (similar to the early Monza 250) and larger 130 mm headlight.

The Sport was a poor man's 100 ohc Sport with jelly mould tank – like the 175 S and 200 Elite – seat from the same source, sprint-type mudguards and four-speed box. In fact it looked a real live sportster, except that it had a puny 5.5 bhp push-rod power unit.

The Bronco was the final model, which first appeared in 1960 expressly for the North American market. Basically an 85 T, but with four speeds, dual-seat and high and wide bars.

1965 Ducati ohv Bronco -- *$379.00

For more information — see a Bronco owner, or your Ducati dealer

Four Speed All Acces. Incl.

America's most popular and reliable lightweight motorcycle. The sturdy four-speed "Bronco", manufactured by the famous Ducati factory in Italy, features numerous engineering refinements usually only found in much more expensive models.

*
F.O.B.
New York:

The 125cc OHV "Bronco" has large full-hub front and rear brakes, steel wheel rims chrome plated, beautifully polished crankcase, tele-draulic front fork, large headlight, tail-stop light, horn, center stand, "jiffy" stand, speedometer, dual-seat and is finished in jet black, silver and chrome and in jet black, candy-apple red and chrome.

BERLINER MOTOR CORPORATION
HASBROUCK HEIGHTS - New Jersey

The American importer's advertisement, proclaiming the merits of the 125 ohv Bronco model, circa 1965.

What to look for

With the possible exception of the 85 Sport, none of these are really worth much effort or expense. And once again you are warned off buying an incomplete example in the hope of finding the missing bits.

Star rating: One star

None of these are likely to get the pulse racing – ever.

Conclusions

All those models, together with the unsuccessful Cruiser scooter, had their roots firmly in the pre-Taglioni Ducati days and should be considered only if you must have a piece of the factory's early history. None are very exciting motorcycles. The exceptions to this are the 98 Sport/Super Sport models. These are collectors' pieces and will become ever more valuable as the years pass by. Also into this category come any *factory* one-offs, like the ISDT models fielded from 1951-54 inclusive, which were powered by versions of the pushrod design, notably the 65 cc unit.

Chapter 3

Gran Sport, Formula 3 and Grand Prix

★ ★ ★ ★ ★	**Gran Sport 1955-57**
★ ★ ★ ★ ★	**F3 125/175 1958-61**
★ ★ ★ ★ ★	**Grand Prix 125 1957-61**
★ ★ ★ ★ ★	**Grand Prix 220 1960**
★ ★ ★ ★ ★	**F3 250 1961-62**

History

Long-distance races over open roads were largely responsible for the development by Ducati, and certain other Italian manufacturers, of very high-performance "sports" machines of low capacity. Regulations for "sports" class racing were first introduced in 1954, but the rules left so many loopholes that they soon needed to be revised.

The 1954 regulations laid down certain conditions, including type approval by the FMI (Italian Motorcycle Federation). An initial 10, followed by another 50, must be built in a year, the price must be constant and as advised to the FMI, caburettor choke sizes were not to exceed those specified by the FMI – ranging from 50 cc two-stroke 17 mm, four-stroke 15 mm, up to 250 cc 30 mm (28 mm). Other requirements included a starting device (usually a kickstarter) and generators for ignition and lighting had to be integral with the power unit.

Although these regulations appeared clear and simple it was not long before certain manufacturers were beating the system. Most famous was the rule regarding carburettors. The regulations stated that the choke could not exceed a certain diameter; so they prepared venturi-shaped chokes, so that the diameter was not constant as intended by the regulations and thus improved induction conditions.

Others announced fantastically high prices, which were, of course, out of the reach of private owners. Moreover, the small manufacturers were ruled out because their limited industrial power did not enable them to produce the minimum number of machines a year.

The result was that in 1956 the regulations were modified. From that time the choke diameter had to be constant and the machine should have no form of streamlining, which had at first been allowed. However, again this didn't prove successful – for example, MV Agusta even fielded one of their 500 cc four-cylinder works racers with streamlining removed and regulation carburettors!

So once again the sport's governing body in Italy sat down and redrafted the regulations. The result was Formula 3 machines, which had to be genuine *production* racers.

Enter Ducati. As described in Chapter 1, Ing. Taglioni's first design for Ducati had been the 100 cc Gran Sport. This had its first airing early in 1955 and later the same season it was joined by an "over-bored" 125 cc version. These bikes were most successful in the marathon long-distance and road races, where other faster machinery usually couldn't stand the pace.

By the end of 1957 the 100 cc model had been abandoned, due in no small part to the banning that year of the very events it was so successful in, the *Giro d'Italia* (Tour of Italy) and the Milano-Taranto, following the Mille Miglia car tragedy.

And for 1958 Ducati concentrated on the

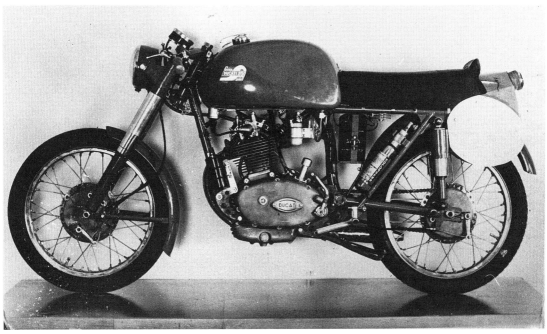

The 100 Gran Sport, forerunner of the Ducati ohc singles, made its début in 1955.

sports machine racing category, whilst still retaining its works participation in the open class.

Gran Sport: 100 and 125 cc, 1955-57
Because the 100 Gran Sport was the ancestor

The 125 Formula 3 racer. Based on the earlier Gran Sport, but with extra tuning and enclosed valve gear.

of all the ohc Ducati singles it is worth a detailed look.

Its' engine had a bore and stroke of 49.4×52 mm giving a capacity of 99.66 cc. The deeply finned light alloy barrel, with reborable cast-iron liner, was inclined forward by 10 degrees — as was the cylinder head. This was also in light alloy, with steel valve seats and featured exposed hairpin valve springs and external oil pipes. The exposed springs were a feature not followed on the models, whether production or racing, which came after the Gran Sport.

The single overhead camshaft was driven by a bevel-shaft on the offside of the engine with straight-cut gears. At the right-hand end of the crankshaft was another pair of straight-cut gears and a shorter bevel-shaft and these were connected to the top section by an Oldham coupling sleeve. Integral teeth on the crankshaft drove both a gear-type oil pump and contact breaker via a large timing gear, and these were all housed within the outer timing cover. The camshaft carried a worm drive for the large white face Veglia rev counter.

The nimonic valves were inclined at 80 degrees and were actuated by short rockers,

Another 125 Formula 3, pictured at Snetterton in August 1963.

One of the earliest 125 Grand Prix models with dual front brake originally intended for use with dustbin fairing.

which were adjusted by means of shim caps. The valve guides were made of phosphor bronze. The same material was used for the small-end bush of the special steel I-shaped connecting rod. The big-end featured caged rollers, while the inside eye of the con-rod acted as the outer bearing surface, with a pressed-up crank-pin for the full-circle crankshaft flywheels.

Primary drive by straight-cut gears and wet multi-plate clutch were on the nearside of the engine unit, as was the kickstarter. Power was transmitted via a four-speed close-ratio gearbox to the rear wheel by a 1/2-in. × 5/16-in. chain.

The Dell'Orto racing carburettor conformed to the FMI ruling and had a remote float which was mounted on a rubber-insulated bracket bolted to the frame. This mounting had a series of holes to allow various positions of adjustment. Also on the left-hand side of the

engine, just inboard of the small primary drive gear on the end of the crankshaft, was a small flywheel magneto supplying current for both the battery of the coil ignition system and the lighting equipment. With an initial power output of 9 bhp at 9,000 rpm the 100 Gran Sport weighed in at 180 lb and was good for just over 80 mph with its "road"-going equipment.

Other important features included a squat racing tank, single seat, 17-in. alloy wheel rims, with 2.50 section tyres, special racing-type − 180 mm front and 160 mm rear − brakes (both single leading-shoe drums), an all-chrome exhaust system − which unlike the production roadsters was flange-bolted to the head, rather than featuring a screwed insert. The top bevel/camshaft cover was secured by four Allen bolts and had the words "Ducati 100 cc Gran Sport" proudly inscribed upon it. This cover was highly polished, unlike the rest of the matt finish engine castings. The bevel-shaft tube was chromed steel − again the production roadster singles which followed had a cast alloy tube.

The finish was an overall deep blood red, with white lettering on the tank. The 125 version, except for its larger 124.89 cc (55.25 × 52 mm) capacity and extra power, 14 bhp at 10,000 rpm giving 87 mph, was identical.

What to look for
Now the bad news, at least for non-Italians. Virtually every Gran Sport was sold in Italy, before the days when the factory had created an export market of any significance, and surviving examples are usually to be found

The GP engine showing the gear train to the dohc.

16

The Ultra Lightweight (125 cc) Isle of Man TT, 3 June, 1959: Australian Ken Kavanagh and his 125 cc Ducati Grand Prix.

within the Italian borders.

Like the other pure limited-run Ducati production racers, the Gran Sports are today extremely valuable – almost on a direct par with classics such as the Manx Norton or AJS 7R. So one in original, fully serviceable condition is going to be *expensive*. Obviously it just might be possible to find one in need of restoration or as a basket case at a cheap figure.

Another problem will be parts, or the lack of them. Much of the Gran Sport was different to its roadster brothers and not just the brake hubs, straight-cut gears or forged piston either. The lighting equipment, kickstarter and other ancillaries are likely to prove even harder to find having been junked long ago when the majority of the bikes were raced in open events during their careers.

Anyone contemplating a GS, otherwise known as the Marianna, needs two things: a supportive bank manager and a lot of patience.

Star rating: Five full stars
The value of this machine is already established and should continue to rise. Even so, if one can find (and afford) an example, I still rate it as a best buy. It is also a superb-looking

miniature motorcycle, a work of mechanical art.

Formula 3: 125 and 175 cc, 1958-61; 250 cc 1961-62
Basically, the Formula 3 models were up-dated versions of the original GS machines with detail improvements, including enclosed valve gear. And in the case of the 175 version a larger capacity and a more powerful front brake. The power output of the 125 F3 was the same as the 125 GS. But the new 175 offered 16 bhp at 9,000 rpm and almost 100 mph (when stripped of its lights, generator and kickstarter). The 174.50 cc (62×57.8 mm) engine shared an identical capacity and dimensions to its roadster version – unlike the smaller bikes.

Although the brakes remained the same for the GS and F3 125s, the 175 had the double-sided Amadoro front stopper and heavily scooped rear brake from the same source. Together with the GP and works Desmo models, the 175/250 F3s were the only Ducatis to use brakes of this type.

All versions of the F3 retained four-speed boxes, and except for the aforementioned enclosed valve gear and different styling were very similar to the original design. There were

17

Daytona, March 1959: American rider Joe Hayes pilots his 175 Formula 3 to second place in the 250 event.

several less obvious changes, such as the different steering head angle, new rear suspension units – those of the original GS models had not always provided the best handling – and a much larger megaphone exhaust.

Although both the Formula 3s were successful in the Italian F3 racing scene – for example, Franco Villa took his 175 to victory in a supporting race at the 1958 Italian Grand Prix at Monza – in pukka racing events they were a lot less competitive. Even so, today they command the same level of aura and desirability as the GS models. One example of the 175 F3 made its way into a moto-crosser in Britain – I wonder what happened to it?

What to look for

Much of what was said for the Gran Sport models applies here – even as far as prices and spare parts. Perhaps the biggest difference is that the F3s were sold abroad, certainly in Europe (including Britain) and the Far East. So the chances of finding an example outside Italy are more likely, although still remote. Advice – snap it up if you get chance. And the 250 F3 was popular and successful in North

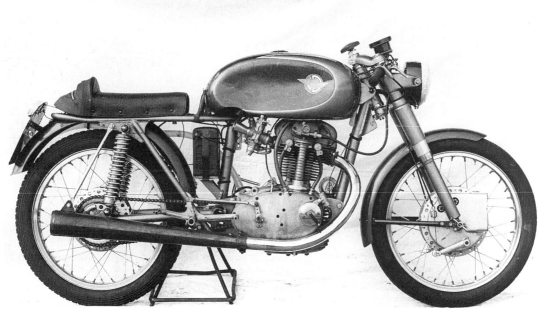

The 175 Formula 3 as it came from the factory, complete with lighting equipment and kickstarter.

America, so examples of these later bikes could well turn up there.

Star rating: Five full stars
For just the same reasons as those given for the Gran Sport!

Grand Prix: 125 cc 1958-61; 220 cc 1960
The Grand Prix had originally been conceived by Ing. Taglioni, as the name implied, as the factory's Grand Prix effort in the ⅛-litre class. But although a fine design it had not proved quite fast enough to challenge the fully streamlined class-leading MV Agustas and FB Mondials.

So when the Desmo 125 single – which after all started life as a Grand Prix with a desmodromic cylinder head – made its race-winning début at the 1956 Swedish GP, the factory's management took the decision to market the dohc design for sale to private owners. This began in 1957, and one of the first foreign owners was Fron Purslow, who made his début on the Bologna machine in March 1958. This same machine was later sold to Stan Hailwood for his son Mike.

Many of the world's top lightweight riders rode a 125 GP Ducati at some stage in their careers. Not only Hailwood, but men like Jim Redman, Tom Phillis, Ken Kavanagh and Dan Shorey, to name but a few. This success was retained until the early 1960s, when faster machines like the Bultaco TSS and Honda CR 93 began to appear.

If the Gran Sport and Formula 3 models had been relatively simple – and cheap, at least in Italy – this could not be said for the Grand Prix. No price was published, as each was virtually hand-built to special order, but in Britain a potential owner could expect to pay somewhere in the region of £1,000 for a used example. This compared with half this figure for a brand new 500 Manx Norton or the 175 Formula 3 Ducati.

Around 50 125 GPs were sold (this figure includes several works Desmo models which were converted to conventional valve spring heads before being sold off during 1959).

Then there was the very rare, larger, 220 version. This came about through Australian Ken Kavanagh (at present resident in Italy), who convinced Taglioni to build him a 250 class

The 175 Formula 3 with which the author began his racing career and which was later raced by Alex George.

bike for use in Australia during the winter of 1959-60. This was achieved by modifying a 175 F3, with double knocker GP-type head and a few other modifications, but still with a four-speed box. The result was a capacity of 216.130 cc (70.5×57.8 mm), which on a 9:1 compression piston gave 28 bhp at 9,600 rpm. Compared to the 125, the 220 offered a considerable improvement in power-to-weight ratio. It showed great potential. Today Kavanagh sees this as "a lost chance."

Although Ducati subsequently built

The extremely rare 220 GP. One of only a handful built, it was based on the 175 Formula 3, but with dohc cylinder head and five speeds.

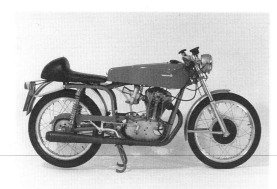

One of a small number of 250/350 Mach 1/S models built in the mid-1960s. In serious racing they were outclassed although they were very reliable.

The 250 Mach 1/S engine. Note the full duplex frame and "wide-case"-type engine. The design was based on the 1964 Barcelona 24-hour race winner.

another four or five examples (with five speeds) they still missed a golden opportunity to cash in during the 1960 season, when the only competitive 250s were either pure factory bikes or the secondhand NSU Sportsmax which cost a small (really big!) fortune. But Ducati let the chance slip. Today there are at least four of these 220s in Britain, but these include the ex-Brian Clark 175 (later 198 cc) F3 which was converted at the factory to 220 cc in 1961. As far as is known no 220 has survived outside Britain.

What to look for
Difficult, as each GP was slightly different to its brother or sister. Some had GS-type brakes, some had double-sided front stoppers – with scoops in various positions! – and a whole variety of frames, including single and double downtube types.

Several GPs ended their racing days in the late 1960s by having Yamaha TD1 two-stroke twin-cylinder engines inserted, with the result that the frame was badly chopped about, whilst others were just broken up or sold for spares. The result is that very few survive today – certainly not many in original condition. Another change to a few examples was the substitution of later Oldani brakes.

Once again spares are extremely hard to find.

Star rating: Five full stars
Except for one of the very few genuine works racers, the Grand Prix is the most collectable – and valuable – of all the Ducatis, certainly any of the singles. These were jewel-like bikes, with the engine built like a watch, and a mass of gears which make the rest of the Ducati family look quite normal by comparison. Most that survive have owners who know their value – and won't sell anyway.

Chapter 4

Strokers

★ ★	48 Sport 1962-65
★ ★	SL1 1967-68
★ ★	125 Regolarita 1975-76
★ ★ ★	125 Six Days 1977
★	Scooters
✦	Other two-strokes

History

Throughout the mid and late-1950s, Ducati Meccanica Spa produced a variety of mopeds and lightweight motorcycles powered by four-stroke engines. Many of these power units were clearly based upon the Cucciolo "clip-on" engine, which had got the factory involved in the two-wheel industry as related in Chapter 2.

But as the 1960s dawned, it was evident that a new formula would be needed, if only because of economic considerations. Quite simply, by then, ultra-lightweight four-strokes had become too expensive to build at a competitive price. And so the saga of the Ducati two-stroke began.

For the entire decade, "strokers" were to prove a vital section of production at the Bologna plant, with a myriad of models for a wide range of purposes: ride to work "step-thru" mopeds, scooters, "café" racer-styled miniature sportsters – even three-wheel delivery trucks! Licence-built variants of the basic design were also constructed at the Spanish Mototrans factory well into the 1970s.

Even though many thousands were built and sold, today many Ducati owners don't even *believe* that the company ever offered anything other than four-strokes!

Brisk and Piuma 1961-67

These were the first models – and were essentially the same except for the number of gears and detail specification. In addition, the 48 cc (38 × 42 mm) engine formed the basis for every Ducati two-stroke thereafter – except the specialized 125 enduro motorcycles of the mid-1970s.

It is also important to realize just how unsophisticated the design really was, with its piston port induction, petroil lubrication and flywheel magneto, which provided power for both the ignition and lighting systems.

The whole purpose of the two-stroke range was to cater for first-time buyers, and in this Ducati were largely successful – until the advent of the much more modern machines from the Orient.

In 1960 the Ducati two-stroke was as good as any other production engine in Europe, but within five short years it was beginning to look thoroughly dated compared to the latest offerings from Japanese manufacturers such as Suzuki and Yamaha. Strangely it was another Japanese manufacturer, Honda, who, had Ducati stuck to their range of under 100 cc four-stroke flyweights, would have found themselves competing against them in the export markets of the world, if they hadn't switched to the two-stroke camp at the small end of the capacity scale.

In its running gear, if not its engine, the Brisk/Piuma mopeds had much in common with Ducati's earlier M55 (see Chapter 2). The pressed-steel frame with integral rear mudguard, swinging arm rear suspension and fuel tank shape were all virtually identical. Only the full-width brake hubs and telescopic front forks were visibly different.

The Brisk was the economy version with single-speed gearbox and a more Spartan specification, whilst the Piuma offered three speeds and an improved level of equipment.

A year after the Brisk/Piuma had first appeared, Deluxe and Sports versions of the latter appeared – with fully enclosed chain and multi-coloured dual-seat – and full motorcycle style respectively.

Compared to the models which followed, the originals were much more successful – with large numbers being constructed over a seven-year period and exported all over the world, even though both were unexciting workhorses.

What to look for

With the quantity produced over a relatively long period, one could be forgiven for thinking that large numbers remain in circulation. In fact very few appear to have survived; not because of any inherent design fault, rather that mopeds tend to be scrapped once their

working life is over, and do not become the source of a restoration project, as a motorcycle might. Even so, some have survived. In fact at the time of writing the author has a 1962 Piuma in his collection.

Parts are a potential problem. Ducati themselves have virtually nothing for these early two-strokes, but, unlike the even earlier push-rod models, the position is not entirely without hope as a few specialist Ducati dealers around the world still have some stocks – it is just a case of knowing who can help, or getting lucky.

But, like other models where spares can be difficult, the best policy is to ensure that the example you intend buying has all the important components such as mudgards, tank, side panels, etc, as locating replacements for these could prove the most difficult. This is obviously made easier when buying a complete machine, rather than a basket case, as in the latter case it is easy to miss something vital which is not there.

A final point to remember is that another Ducati moped, very similar to the Brisk, was offered in 1968. This was the Rolly, a single-

A 1962 illustration of the three-speed Piuma moped. Capable of 200 mpg, it sold in Britain for £68.

22

speed machine with an unsprung frame. Its lack of success can be measured by its short production life of barely 12 months.

Star rating: One charitable star
Remember these are the basic mopeds. Their single-star rating is conferred because they were the first of the line.

48 Sport 1962-65
Capable of almost 50 mph, the 48 Sport (known as the Falcon in North America) was a genuine motorcycle in miniature, with its sturdy twin-cradle frame, 19-in. wheels and racing lines. Strangely it largely failed to attract customers, even though it received a good press.

Launched in the spring of 1962, it *should* have been a commercial success. Maybe a reason it didn't is contained in this extract from the 27 June, 1963, issue of *The Motor Cycle:* "It *looks* like many Italian 50s and yet it has charm and character all its own." In other words it didn't *look* different enough. It wasn't expensive to buy – under £90 in 1963; or to run – well over 100 mpg.

So why didn't it sell? Other than that stated above, the answer probably is that whilst riders had accepted both mopeds and scooters, they (except in Italy) had not ac-

cepted anything much less than 100 cc as a motorcycle in the early 1960s. Again, within a few short years the Japanese were to change all this . . . helped by a large publicity campaign and machines of high performance (like the Ducati 48 Sport) and accessories such as flashing indicators, oil pump lubrication, chrome mudguards and even electric starting on some models (unlike the Ducati!). Also offered was an 80 cc version, but this proved even less successful than the smaller bike and was soon dropped.

Star rating: Two stars
The 48 Sport, together with the SL1 and later 125 enduro models, is the most collectable of the Ducati two-strokes. With that said, I can't visualize it ever becoming anything more than interesting, and not a serious vehicle for investment purposes.

Brio scooters 1963-68
The Ducati management had witnessed the huge success of the Lambretta and Vespa scooters. It should also have taken note of its earlier costly blunder with the overweight, underpowered Cruiser scooter of the early 1950s. Sadly it didn't! The result was the range of Brio scooters with capacities of 48 and 94 cc. These were powered by identical engines to

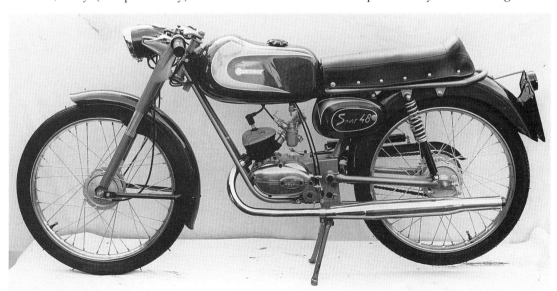

The 48 Sport (Falcon in North America). This miniature sportster featured a full duplex frame, clip-ons and a top speed of around 50 mph. It was available from 1962 to 1965.

the mopeds and lightweight motorcycles, but featuring exclusively fan-cooling and three speeds for their whole life.

The introduction of these machines was too late. By 1963 the scooter boom was all but over, and in any case the Ducati offerings had smaller-capacity engines than the successful Lambretta and Vespa models.

What to look for
One word: Don't! These were unwanted then, and equally so today, so stay well clear.

Star rating: A miserable half star!
Nothing else worth saying.

Cadet and Mountaineer 1964-67
Ducati's attempt to offer 100 cc class road and trail bikes. Although reasonably successful in their day, they were soon upstaged and outclassed by the Japanese onslaught in world markets.

It's also difficult to conclude if these were built for America, the general export market, or even Italy – although the first seems the most likely.

When they were launched in 1964 the feature most noticable was the fan-cooling,

identified by the large alloy dome over the head and barrel, driven by a finned plate bolted on to the flywheel magneto rotor on the offside of the engine.

Essentially the two machines – Cadet (also known in USA as Falcon 100) (roadster) and Mountaineer (on-off road) – were mechanically the same, but to suit their differing roles they had various changes to seating, gearing, handlebars, exhaust, tyres and other smaller details. Both machines shared a chrome-plated rear carrier as standard equipment and three-speed hand-operated (as on the 48 Sport and Piuma) twistgrip gearchange.

1966 saw both models gain a four-speed, foot-operated gearchange. This was a definite improvement over the original.

A year later they were up-dated yet again. This time there was a capacity increase of 1 mm to 52 mm, giving 98 cc. In the process the fan-cooling and iron cylinder barrel had been dispensed with, their place being taken by a massively finned alloy cylinder barrel, with flash chromed bore. There was also a matching head, with corresponding deeper finning. Performance was notably improved, with maximum speed increasing from 60 to 65 mph.

Ducati's attempt to cash in on the scooter boom, the Brio, was available in 50 cc and 100 cc engine sizes. It was too late and few were sold.

Also in 1967 a *four-stroke* model (with push-rod operated valves) appeared, known as the Cadet/4, in three guises: Standard, Lusso and Scrambler. These are included in this chapter as only the top end of the engine and some styling changes place them apart from the smaller two-stroke versions!

At the end of 1967 all Cadet (and Mountaineer) models were discontinued.

What to look for
Over 95 per cent of the Cadet and Mountaineer models manufactured were the original 94 cc fan-cooled type. So the later 98 cc two-stroke and 125 cc Cadet/4 are much rarer – and therefore spares, which are different for the original models, are even more difficult, if not impossible, to locate. In addition the barrel of the 98 cc two-stroke cannot be rebored.

Star rating: One single star
The only real interest of the Cadet or Mountaineer models is the chance to own a Ducati motorcycle (as opposed to a moped or scooter)

at a low cost. But compared to the Japanese machines of the same capacity which followed they are primitive.

SL Series 1964-69
These were ultra-lightweight motorcycles which replaced the 48 Sport. The first of the series, the 1964-65 48 SL (Sport Lusso) used the fan-cooled engine (but suitably tuned) from the 48 Brio scooter. Depending on the market, it was also sold under the *Cacciotore* name in Italy and as the Falcon in North America.

In 1966 the 48 SL became the 50 SL, fan-cooling was dispensed with and the capacity raised 2 cc from 47.5 to 49.5 mm by enlarging the cylinder bore by .8 mm, and as on the larger two-stroke engine on the Cadet/Mountaineer models, the barrel was substituted with an alloy one with a chrome bore. At the same time a four-speed foot-operated gear-change was incorporated.

A year later and the SL/1 was introduced. For the first time since the 48 Sport, Ducati had chosen "café racer" styling. This meant

The fan-cooled Mountaineer: built in three- and four-speed forms it was a trail version of the Cadet roadster, which was available at the same time.

25

clip-on bars, a long slim and shapely tank capped by *twin* fillers (as on the first batch of Desmo singles), a single seat and exposed suspension springs fore and aft – which combined to produce a most attractive sporting flyweight.

The following year the final variations appeared. The SL1/A and SL/2 were in contrast strictly touring models, with none of the distinctive racer styling of their predecessor – indeed in my opinion a backward step. These proved unpopular, and the final SL, a /2 left the factory's production lines in 1969.

What to look for
Except for the stylish SL/1, not much to commend them, other than as cheap transport – and in that role there are a lot of more practical, better machines around. A handful of SL/1s were converted into club racers by British importer Vic Camp.

Star rating: SL/1 two stars, the others one star
That sculptured twin filler cap tank of the SL/1 is worth two stars alone.

50/100 Scrambler 1969-70
Like the Brio scooters before them, the 50/100 Scramblers (not the real thing!) were seen by the factory's management as a way of cashing in on a perceived "boom" market, only this time it wasn't scooters but the dirt bike craze sweeping Italy at the time. And like the Brios before them, the Scramblers were unsuccessful, soon fading away after poor sales.

These two models utilized the engine and frame assemblies of the early 50 and 100 class motorcycles. In addition they were kitted out with a fresh style to match their intended task, which included a pair of exposed Ceriani-pattern front forks. Probably because there were very few new parts or mechanics, Ducati didn't lose too much money from R and D costs.

What to look for
Again hardly worth the effort – quite simply didn't match up to the name.

Star rating: One star – just
Can't think of a suitable – printable – word to

The 50 SL/1 which replaced the 48 Sport as Ducati's offering in the 50 cc sportster class.

describe just how mediocre these really were.

125 Regolarita 1975-76

This was yet another attempt by Ducati to win a new breed of customer, and like the majority before it destined to prove very much a failure.

By the mid-1970s it was fashionable for Italians (or at least the well-heeled type) to be seen riding a pukka enduro mount on the road. So of course Ducati felt they needed such a machine, even though they had no experience of building one for sale to the public. The result was the Regolarita, but as several observers were later to note it had a problem right from the start – identified perfectly in an article in *On Two Wheels*, which said: "The name Ducati is associated with a special breed of Italian road and racing machines each of which is light, beautifully made and exceptionally quick. Therefore, some might find it surprising that the Bologna company also pro-

duces a neat 125 cc, two-stroke six-day-trial-cum-road machine. In fact, the Ducati does suffer from something of an identity crisis."

Sadly this was all too true. Not only was it expensive (at least twice as much as a conventional roadster or trial bike of the same capacity), but it also had been given the dual roles of a road *and* enduro racing motorcycle – an impossible task – and this showed, as although it was well made and featured a list of quality components it was not particularly successful in either of its appointed tasks. It was too heavy for competition use and too highly strung for road use . . . needless to say a modular range of not only 125 but 175 and 250 versions never saw the light of day, due to its lack of showroom success.

What to look for

This is a rare bird, both in Britain and North America – or for that matter anywhere outside its homeland. In Italy few survived due to

The mid-1970s saw Ducati make a return to two-strokes with the six-speed 125 Regolarita. It suffered something of an identity crisis –

customers expected sporting roadsters, not off-road dirt irons . . .

Ducati's final stroker – the 1977 Six Days. Although a full-blown enduro motorcycle with the finest equipment, it still failed to prove a sales success.

the ageing process of obsolete dirt bikes, but unlike other failures already mentioned in this chapter, I reckon that the Regolarita may well become a sought after model – but wouldn't like to place bets on it. Watch out for its Achilles' heel, a wrecked gearbox if used in serious competition.

Star rating: Two stars
Worth a two-star rating on rarity and quality of component parts alone.

125 Six Days 1977
An attempt to create a full-blown enduro, after the "half-way-house" Regolarita, the Six Days was a single-minded competition bike. Gone were all pretensions of a dual-purpose motorcycle. In its place a pukka fire-breathing enduro racing iron.

A much improved and revised engine now gave 25 bhp (against the 21.8 of the earlier bike). This was mounted in a heavily modified frame, which now featured a revised tubular swinging arm (previously in square section)

with the rear shocks laid down at an acute angle. Other changes included stronger forks, a moto-cross-style exhaust system, a new alloy petrol tank and revised plastic ware.

Even though it was a superior machine, well suited to its purpose, a change in factory planning saw the Six Days dropped. This also spelled the end of a full racing moto-cross version, which had reached the advanced prototype stage.

What to look for
By the time the Six Days was ready for production the factory's management (under siege at the time from their government bosses in far off Rome) had come to realize that there were other priorities more important than a company presence in the specialized field of enduro racing. Therefore after the first batch no more Six Days were produced. You will be lucky if you find one in Italy – and it is almost impossible outside.

Star rating: Three solid stars
Even rarer than the Regolarita – and much more suitable for off-road use. The only question over the machine is that like all dirt bikes, however good, they are made obsolete by next year's crop of machinery. In Ducati's case this may prove different if the Six Days becomes a sought after classic at some stage in the future.

Summary
So there you have it, the vast range of Ducati two-strokes, why they appeared and why they didn't make it in a bigger way. I doubt very much if there will be another two-stroke from Bologna in the near future, unless it's a badge engineered Cagiva. But for over a decade in the company's history they played an important commercial role – broadening the model line and earning additional revenue.

Chapter 5

Narrow-case Singles

★ ★ ★	175 and 200
★ ★ ★	250s (except Mach 1)
★ ★ ★ ★	Mach 1
★ ★	All other models

History

All the ohc singles covered in this chapter are "narrow-case" models – those where the front *and* rear engine mountings are of the same width. Equally, all were directly derived from the sports/racer models described in Chapter 3, which in turn were designer Ing. Taglioni's first for his new employers, when he joined the Bologna company in the mid-1950s.

The first of the ohc production roadsters was the 175 Sport (known as the Silverstone in Britain), which made its début at the 1956 Milan Show.

This was quickly followed by a vast array of differing models – but all with the same basic engine layout – in 100, 125, 200 and, of course, 175 cc capacities.

1961 saw the introduction of the all-important 250. Then in 1964 a 160 and finally, in 1965, a 350.

Essentially the 100, 125 and 160 were in one family, the 175, 200, 250 and 350 in another. Although all shared the same basic bevel-driven single overhead camshaft layout, with wet sump lubrication and full unit construction.

As *Cycle World* said in an early test, the engine "is the outstanding feature." On all these models it was an all-alloy single with a cobby, purposeful look. The neat appearance was due to its classic, timeless lines and superb castings. This was heightened by an absence of oil leaks (something which many machines of the era couldn't boast) and the exclusive use of recessed, Allen screws in place of the traditional cap-screws.

The finning around the cylinder barrel and head was deep, giving an almost "road racer" look – which wasn't surprising once one realizes its history.

Inside the engine was just as exciting. A double-flywheel, pressed-up crankshaft was used, but with the addition of a built-in sludge trap and large screw. The oil was fed into the offside end of the crank (which ran in a bronze bush) and led out into a chamber in the rim of the flywheel before flowing back to the passage leading to the crankpin bearing. There was also a more conventional gauze filter integral with the oil drain plug located in the base of the crankcases.

The engine's single overhead cam was driven by bevel gears and tower shafts, split in the middle and joined by an Oldham's coupling – very much like the classic single-cam Norton engine.

Rockers (with either lock nuts or shims depending on the model) transmitted power from the cam lobes to the valves, and the valves themselves were closed by means of hairpin springs.

Unlike pure racing models such as the GS and GP, these springs were entirely enclosed in the cylinder head casting. Phosphor bronze was widely used throughout the engine, including valve guides and rocker bushes.

The gear selector mechanism was housed in a quickly detachable assembly on the offside of the engine, whilst there was helical-geared primary drive, and a wet multi-plate clutch.

It was details like this which added up to such a formidable and effective design – certainly by the standards of the day.

Likewise the simple but effective chassis. The frame used the engine as a stressed member, and once again phosphor bronze was used for the swinging arm pivot bushes.

Although offering a much more rigid set-up than the more commonly used metalastic bushes, the bronze components were prone to wear rapidly unless lubricated on a regular basis.

Wheel hubs and suspension were "brought in" – usually from Grimeca and Marzocchi, respectively.

Over the years the Ducati singles proved themselves extremely versatile, being used for a truly amazing number of roles, from sedate touring to moto-cross racing and everything in between.

100, 125, 175 and 200

Of these, except for the 200, very few seem to have survived. This is not because they were the earliest of the line, but because they were often owned by less than caring raw novices. These riders were simply not in a position to appreciate what jewel-like bikes these tiny Bologna machines really were. Those that did survive often ended their days on the race track; for example, the British importers at the time, Ducati Concessionaires (alias Kings of Manchester), offered racing kits for the 125, 175 and 200 models. The smallest model was not imported until the end of 1959.

I will therefore concentrate on the 200. The early version made up to the beginning of 1961 was in reality simply a bored-out 175 – from 62 to 67 mm – the stroke remaining identical at 57.8 mm, but by then the 175 and 100 had all but disappeared. However, even though the 250 appeared in the spring of that year, the 200 (and 125) continued until the middle of the decade, although from early 1961 the 200 engine was based on the 250 rather than the 175 unit.

A distinctive failure of most 200s was the exhaust system. This employed a single pipe running into a "Y"-branch with two Silentium silencers. This might have been all right for styling, but it was hardly practical – not only was there the extra cost of two silencers, but stacked one above the other the system was prone to grounding, particularly when carrying a pillion passenger.

The 200 (actually 203.783 cc) was good for around 85 mph in Elite or Super Sport roadster trim. On paper this was identical to the 175 Sport's 84 mph (although tuned versions of the 175 offered 10 mph more). But with its extra torque the larger engine was more practical for normal use.

Other 200 models included the US-custom Americano and Moto-cross.

Compared with rival lightweights of their day the various early narrow-case models offered exceptional performance, outstanding roadholding and powerful brakes. In contrast some of the finish (paintwork and chrome) was lousy, and bikes made much better sport-

This Classic bevel-driven ohc Ducati single is a 248 cc Mach 1 of 1965 vintage.

30

sters than tourers – a trend which was followed by later models from the factory.

Engine reliability was also good *provided* that the engine was used in a sporting manner and not allowed to slog in too high a gear – and that it received regular oil changes (at around 1,500 miles). Unfortunately, more often than not the owner did just the reverse. The result was a spate of big-end failures which took the marque years to live down. As proof of this, in the rigours of racing, the engine proved almost unburstable.

250

The first 250 was based around a bored-out 175 Formula 3 racer which was campaigned by works rider Francesco Villa (brother of three times 250 World Champion Walter) in North America during 1960. Like so much of Ducati's racing, this bike acted as a prototype for the roadster line.

In early 1961, Ducati released two brand-new production models, the Monza tourer and the Diana sportster, both sharing the same 248 cc (74 × 57.8 mm) four-speed engine. The Monza had a softer cam, smaller-capacity tank, high bars, a deeper seat padding, a prop-stand and a deeply valanced rear mudguard.

The Diana (known in Britain as the Daytona) came equipped with clip-ons, a larger and more attractive fuel tank, a narrower, largely unpadded seat and narrow-section mudguards front and rear.

Surprisingly, except for the cam profile, both engines were identical, and both shared the same 24 mm Dell'Orto UFB carburettor. Performances were similar: 80 mph for the Monza, 85 mph for the Diana.

However, with a larger carburettor – a 27 mm Dell'Orto SS racing-type – and the addition of a higher compression piston (the standard Diana and Monza shared an 8:1 four-ring type) plus a racing megaphone, a performance in excess of 100 mph was possible, making the Diana a popular choice for budget road racers on both sides of the Atlantic.

The 200 Elite introduced in 1959 proved to be a success on both track and road around the world.

Note the double barrel silencer and "jelly mould" tank.

250 Daytona (Diana), Ducati's first production 250. It was introduced in May 1961 and a racing kit boosted its maximum speed to around 100 mph.

Even in standard trim the Diana was impressive – and as the owner of one way back in 1961-62 I should know. Quite simply, except for the Honda CB72, it was the fastest thing on the road in its class – and quite able to humiliate bikes twice its size. With the race kit fitted it was unbeatable!

Besides the performance, its roadholding, braking and engine smoothness gained top marks. The riding position was also good – even though the seat always appeared on the hard side. Gearbox and clutch were excellent, except for a tendency to select false neutrals, and sometimes it proved difficult to obtain neutral at a standstill.

The clip-ons featured welded brackets, so the controls could not be adjusted for position – an annoying point. I always found my machine a first-time starter – and (with 24 mm carburettor), fuel consumption *never* dropped below 60 mpg, and quite often approached 80 mpg!

The Daytona sold in Britain from May 1961 to late 1964, by which time it had been completely outpaced by the much more potent Mach 1.

One of the last road tests carried out was by *Motor Cycle* in their 14 May, 1964, issue. They concluded by saying: "Waving goodbye to the Ducati Daytona was a sad occasion. Whether pottering around town or steaming up the M1 it was in its element; a machine of which the

Most of the early Ducati ohc singles came with clip-on bars which gave them a distinct café racer style.

32

Italian industry should be proud."

It has to be said that in many ways the Daytona was a much more practical, smoother machine than the fire-breathing ton-up Mach 1 super sportster which replaced it, even though it wasn't as quick.

But before looking at this model, there was another four-speeder to complete the trio. This was the Scrambler (not sold in Britain) – not really a serious moto-cross racer but more a bike which could compete in various sporting events, at least in the North America of the early 1960s.

The American importers called the Scrambler a "four-in-one" machine, claiming that it could – with a change of tyres – manage street riding, road racing, short-track racing and scrambles.

To be honest it was really master of none. As a roadster it was none too successful, even if you fitted a silencer instead of its open pipe, due to a skimpy seat, small mudguards, weak flywheel-driven magneto electrics and knobbly tyres.

For road racing it was a better bet to start with a Diana. As a short-track racer it was probably at its best, but even then was outpaced by the purpose-built racers. And for serious dirt use . . . *Cycle World,* August, 1962: "When

the going gets really nasty, the bike's wheelbase, fork angle and suspension are not precisely what one might call ideal."

Cycle World concluded that: "Those pumpkin sized clods that are a standard feature for some cross-country courses might be too much for the Ducati's essentially road-going frame and forks."

Even so the Scrambler sold well in the States, and was the forerunner of the factory's top-selling wide-case Street Scrambler of the late 1960s and early 1970s. *Cycle World* put their 250 Scrambler through the speed trap at 82 mph and the standing quarter-mile in 17.3 secs – 73 mph.

September 1964 saw the launch of the hottest narrow-case single of all, the much-vaunted 250 Mach 1. Shortly after, *Motor Cycle* began their road test in the 5 November, 1964, issue by saying: "Without doubt, the Italian Ducati Mach 1 is the fastest production 250 ever tested by *Motor Cycle.* Although it would not pull its 5.39-to-1 top gear to advantage on MIRA's fairly short timing straight, this fifth speed would take the bike over the 100 mph mark on the motorway. Geared for 115 mph, the bike will fulfil the manufacturer's claim of 106 mph, given neutral conditions and the rider glued to the tank like a pancake on

When it appeared in 1964, the 250 Mach 1 was the fastest machine in its class. Today its the most sought-after ''narrow-case'' model with collectors and enthusiasts alike.

the ceiling. Forgetting top gear, though, the 97 mph best one-way speed in fourth is creditable enough."

In designing the Mach 1 Ducati clearly put performance right at the top. Compared to the previous models this engine had a higher-compression 3-ring piston, fiercer cam profile, larger valves, stronger hairpin springs, a larger inlet port and a 29 mm Dell'Orto SS1 29D carburettor and a five-speed gearbox to complete the impressive specification.

All this added up to a performance ideally suited to the race track or high-speed road work – but town work was definitely not one of its favourites. *Motor Cycle* said: "The Ducati Mach 1 is nothing less than a fully-fledged clubman racer with lights added as an afterthought."

Unlike the early models, which had clip-ons, the newcomer had the full treatment,

with rear set footrests and controls. Unfortunately, the curved kickstart lever was almost impossible as a starting device.

And although, as usual, the performance, handling, braking and rideability received top marks, the electrics most certainly didn't, even though the output had increased over the old four-speed engine from 40 to 60 watts.

On this subject *Motor Cycle* said: "Lighting is definitely below par for a 100 mph sportster. The headlamp emits only a yellowish beam; this is not satisfactory by any means."

Motor Cycling also tested the very same Mach 1 – registration number GEV 156B – in their 27 February, 1965, issue. They found it "grossly overgeared." I would fully agree with this, as the original 18 × 40 gearing is the very highest of both gearbox and rear wheel sizes available. And they adjudged the lights to be "about as effective as a candle."

Many Mach 1s were converted into racers, even, when new, and this 1965 photograph of a "racerised" Vic Camp example proves the point.

34

In many ways – except for cubic capacity – the Mach 1 was closest to a DBD34 Clubman's BSA Gold Star. For a start both were the top sporting roadster single of their era. Both were bikes with a definite Clubman's racer image, both were difficult in traffic, real pigs to start and only really happy out on the open road, and neither were really effective against pukka racing machinery on the track. Finally both are today in high demand among classic enthusiasts, and a long way in front of their more staid and largely far more sensible, but less glamorous sisters.

Of course, like the BSA, there were other 250 Ducatis available at the same time as the Mach 1 – the GT (called Daytona GT in Britain), Monza and Scrambler, the latter two being "new" five-speed versions which replaced the original models following the release of the Mach 1.

Compared to the out-and-out sportster, the GT, Monza and even the Scrambler had performances which were mild in comparison. For example, the GT was tested by *Motor Cycle* and was found to have a *true* maximum speed of only 74 mph. But against this, each were far easier to live with and in any case could, and

were, tuned to Mach 1 standard by anyone wishing to convert his into a fast roadster or clubman racer.

Then there was the five-speed Diana, more commonly known as the *Mark* (and not Mach) *3*. In 1964-65 this was a sort of half-way house between the touring models and the Mach 1. But for 1966 the Mark 3 received the full Mach 1 treatment, and then, in 1967 (its final year of production), it took the place of the Mach 1, which was dropped. It should be noted that American Mark 3s usually came with flywheel magnetos and no battery, whereas European spec. models were identical to the Mach 1 with a generator and battery.

The vast majority of Monzas and Mark 3s wouldn't have made it to Britain, except for a whole shipment of 3,500 machines that was refused by the American importer (the Berliner Motor Corporation of New Jersey). Together with 160 Monza Juniors, 350 Sebrings and a few 100 Cadet ultra-lightweight motorcycles and Brio scooters, the whole shipment was purchased by Bill Hannah of Liverpool and distributed throughout Britain from 1968 to 1972.

Motorcycle Mechanics tested a couple of these

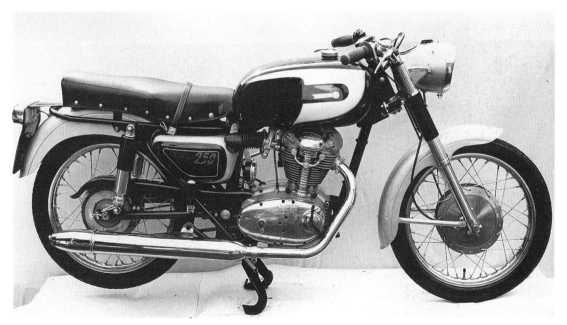

The 250 GT tourer was part of Ducati's five-speed ohc range. It was sold as the Daytona GT in Britain.

35

bikes – a Mark 3 and 250 Monza – in their September 1969 issue, saying that they were "value for money" and that "racing improves the breed." Prices were at least 25 per cent less than that charged by official importer Vic Camp. But in the real world these were "old", replaced by the wide-case models described in Chapter 6.

350 Sebring

An oddball one this: although it was the largest of the narrow-case singles, it was by no means the quickest. In reality it was a five-speed 250 Monza with a larger bore *and* stroke – 76 × 76 mm, giving a capacity of 340 cc.

In standard trim, with the 24 mm Dell'Orto UBF carburettor (same size as the 200s!), the Sebring was a poor performer, just creeping over the 80 mph mark. And unlike the 250 it tended to have a nasty habit of kicking back when being started. This usually resulted in either a badly bruised leg or a broken gear on the kickstart quadrant. In all other respects it

was the same as the equivalent year's Monza, but like all the other singles it could be made to perform much better with a larger (usually 30 or 32 mm) carburettor, 350 Desmo piston and a green/white camshaft. These, plus the larger valves and stronger springs from the Mach 1, were guaranteed to make it fly. Converted Sebrings have performed well in road racing events, both on the short circuit and long races such as the Isle of Man Manx GP.

160 Monza Junior

One thousand five hundred, almost half, of the Hannah shipment were 160s. This meant that there are, even to this day, lots of them in Britain. The press thought it one of the best Ducatis ever, but the buying public didn't agree, so this meant sales were never anything other than poor, even when the price was heavily discounted. This was because Ducati enthusiasts (buyers!) tended to go for sport-sters – hence the fame of the Mach 1.

A "narrow-case" 250 Mark 3 in action at the 1968 Barcelona 24-hour race. Rider Reg Everett, together with co-pilot Paul Smart came home third overall, a super achievement.

36

The square-styled 1966 340 cc Sebring was
Ducati's largest single at the time. Its performance
in standard trim was disappointing.

The original version of 160 Monza Junior clearly
aimed at the American tourist, rather than the
European sports rider.

By comparison the 160 was purely a touring ride-to-work mount – even though it had that classic ohc engine. *Motorcycle Sport's* tester called it: "One of the most impressive small motorcycles I have ever ridden," whilst *Motor Cycle* summed the 160 up well: "The sit-up riding position and large, well-padded dual-seat bring this machine out of the traditional Ducati rut of Spartan comfort. Unlike the ultra-sporting versions of this single-cylinder engine, that of the Monza 160 is remarkably tractable and fuss-free. Starting is first kick every time provided the carburettor is lightly flooded."

That last statement is absolutely true. The one I owned in the early 1970s was such a reliable starter that I would take bets on it starting first time hot or cold! I even went to the 1972 Manx GP on it when a certain British machine of much larger capacity broke down on the way there. The little Ducati got me there and back in a completely fuss-free fashion and at minimum expense – fuel consumption was amazingly frugal, between 110-130 mpg. The maximum speed was a timed 72 mph. And of the "square"-styled singles (250 Monza, 350 Sebring and 160), the smallest bike looked by far the nicest.

But once again the 160 gained a poor reputation in its early days – when purchased as a cheap means of transport and thrashed with virtually nil servicing. Also the factory got it wrong and the majority of bikes – certainly as regards the Hannah shipment – were undergeared, which led to problems with shattered main bearings and valves dropping in.

Summary
All narrow-case models tend to be more fragile than the later wide-case types. This was particularly highlighted when the machines didn't get the maintenance, including regular oil changes, which their unit construction and usually high state of engine tune demanded.

Against the superb alloy castings, racer-like handling, braking and engine performance, were a number of glaring faults such as poor

Before restoration . . .

38

. . . and after: a 1966 Ducati 160 Monza Junior
Series 3. The megaphone silencer is non-standard.

paintwork and chrome, weak and often unreliable electrics and lack of attention to detail.

Today, as always, many Ducatis are used on the track. Here the narrow-case engine and frame offer a combination which has a more effective power-to-weight ratio than the later wide-case type, but for serious use the 31.5 mm front forks and single-sided drum brake are completely outclassed. My advice is to fit the later dual drum brake and the stronger 35 mm Marzocchi forks from the 73/74 Mark 3.

Also, except possibly for the 160 Monza Junior, the narrow-case singles are most certainly not ride-everyday machines. That's why over the years they have proved more popular as racers than roadsters.

Star ratings

The Mach 1 earns the highest score in this section, not because it is the most practical bike, but because it is the most glamorous.

But before you buy a Mach 1, make sure it's the real thing. For a start the engine number should read DM250M1 (Mark 3 reads DM250M3 and the Sebring DM350S). Without this prefix it's a Monza, GT or similar. Also the Mach 1 was the only Bologna-built narrow-case ohc 250 to have a red frame. The Diana (Daytona) had a metallic blue or black frame and the Mark 3, Monza, GT and Scrambler all had black frames.

There are very few *genuine* road-going Mach 1s around. In Britain most were built into racers, many from new by importer Vic Camp, and anyone wishing to construct a Mach 1 roadster out of a racer will have a difficult task, as the road bits to complete the conversion (mudguards, toolboxes, tank and seat) have long since been unavailable.

If you are seeking to buy a Ducati ohc single *cheaply*, the 160 Monza Junior is definitely the best bet. These are still easy to find *and* cheap. How long this will remain so is difficult to tell, but I suspect shorter rather than longer.

I know I had lots of fun on my 160, so don't be put off by what you may have previously been told – but at the same time don't expect ton-up performance.

Chapter 6

Wide-Case Singles

★ ★	Street Scramblers
★ ★ ★	Mark 3s
★ ★ ★ ★	All Desmo models

History

After over a decade in production, the Ducati bevel-driven overhead cam singles, in their various forms, had shown the factory that they were in need of improvement in certain vital areas of design. The first of the production models had gone on sale in early 1957 and been produced in a wide range of capacities from 98 to 340 cc. Towards the end of the 1960s Ducati realized that something would have to be done to re-launch the theme and the result was a new family of singles, owing much in their basic concept to the original models.

The feature which most easily identified these new-era machines was the frame, which is known today as the "wide-case"-type. This is because, unlike all the earlier production models, it is characterized by having the rear engine mounting bolts and crankcase mountings some four times wider than the front ones, whereas on the original, all were the same "narrow-case" width.

In many ways the "prototype" of the new models was the small batch of endurance racing replicas in 250 and 350 cc capacities constructed by Ducati in 1965, following their success in the 1964 Barcelona 24 Hours Race. Sold under the Mach 1/S banner these relative heavyweights proved ultra-reliable, but on short circuits they were totally uncompetitive.

There the whole thing might well have rested, except for one thing, Ing. Taglioni's love of racing and his knowledge that if nothing else it was an "unofficial" way to get a new production project under way. But Taglioni realized that the narrow-case singles were rapidly becoming dated, and he wanted to finally exploit his Desmodromic technology on the production front.

So began a very low-profile racing operation. For this Taglioni enlisted the services of riders Gilerto Parlotti and Roberto Gallina, and it was the latter who rode the first 350 single-cylinder Desmo on its inaugural outing at Modena in March 1967. This proved a success, as Gallina finished well up the field in both the 350 and 500 classes.

After more successful appearances, during which time a 250 was built, Taglioni achieved a long-held ambition – the authorization of desmo valve operation for production machines – and at the same time a redesign of his original bevel-driven single-cylinder model range.

The first the public saw of the new roadsters was at the vast bi-annual show at Cologne in West Germany, held during September 1967. The model displayed at Cologne was a 350 (actually, like the narrow-case Sebring, 340 cc), and known as the Mark 3. But surprisingly, perhaps, Ducati opted to make the first production batch employing the wide-case frame and engine as Street Scramblers, known as the SCR, in 350 engine size.

They were soon followed by both Mark 3 and Desmo versions: the wide-case production run had begun.

SCR (Street Scramblers) 1968-74
Besides the wider rear engine mounts the new frame was much stronger at the rear, and compared to the strictly roadster Mark 3 and Desmo models the front forks were longer and

more robust – and both these and the rear suspension units carried rubber gaiters.

In general style they were very much like the narrow-case 250 Scrambler offered between 1962-67, but there was now the addition of a new tank, with chrome side panels, high-and-wide unbraced "bars", a larger air filter,

The first "wide-case" single to enter production was the Scrambler (SCR) in May 1968, available at first in 250 and 350 engine sizes.

41

A proud Norwegian owner with his slightly modified 1973 350 Scrambler.

short, dumpy silencer with slashed end cone and other smaller differences.

But besides the new frame, it was the engine which had seen the biggest up-date, with attention finally being paid to the previous weak spots, such as kickstart gears, main bearings and crankshaft (although initially the crankpin size remained at 27 mm).

The first 350 SCRs were released in early 1968, not only going on sale in Italy but also in the USA, where the model was known as the 350 SS (Street Scrambler).

Later that year a smaller quarter-litre version was released. Both the 250 and 350 retained the bore and stroke measurements of the earlier models.

Then early the following year came a completely new capacity model, the 450, actually 436 cc (86×75 mm). Like the 350 this used a valve lifter. There were a number of changes made, which included bracing the frame's top

The 1974 450 Scrambler sold in Britain as the "Mark 4". Note the non-standard silencer, Amal Concentric Mark 1 carburettor and Lucas headlight.

42

tube, wider chain and sprockets, taller exhaust pipe (to match an increase in cylinder barrel height) and – one which didn't show up in any specification sheet – considerable vibration. It's something of a trade-off; for this disadvantage, the larger engine offered considerably more torque, if not outright top end power. And because of this the 450 was at its best in SCR form.

Unlike the pure roadster, the SCRs remained virtually unchanged until the very last – except for the final 350 and 450 versions, which shared many parts – such as brakes, forks, instruments and lighting equipment with the final Mark 3 in 1973-74.

Also during 1971 a new model had made its bow. This was the 125 Scrambler, which used a Spanish-built engine assembly and (unlike the earlier Italian engine) had a five-speed box. It also used the old narrow-case frame, with modern Marzocchi exposed stanchion forks. Largely this was a failure, at least from a sales point of view, as its price was almost that of the larger models, and it was soon dropped

The 1972 450 Mark 3 touring model still retained old 31.5 mm enclosed forks.

from production.

What to look for

For a start it may come as a suprise, but the Street Scramblers easily outsold the Mark 3 and Desmo models on the home market. And furthermore, in an interview in 1988, the legendary Ducati designer Ing. Fabio Taglioni

The 1974 350 Mark 3 blue and gold model with 35 mm Marzocchi forks and double drum front brake. Most bikes came with clip-ons as illustrated.

mentioned them as being among his favourite designs. All this will probably come as a shock to readers who regard the café racer-styled sports roadsters, such as the Mach 1 and Desmos, as the real Bologna one-lungers.

Also in markets such as Britain, the SCRs were never imported in anything more than small batches.

The SCRs are best described as "shooting, fishing and hunting"-type machines, rather than as serious dirt irons such as moto-crossers, enduros or even trail bikes.

Combined with their *ride-anywhere ability* was a higher level of reliability than on the previous singles and the increased strength of several components. Also one has to bear in mind that the Italian market was "protected" – the importation of Japanese motorcycles were largely banned – so the SCRs with their wide range of usage appealed to a captive market, deprived of state-of-the-art Oriental small and mid-range bikes.

Star rating: Two stars
Times have changed, the Ducati singles in de-

mand with "Classic" enthusiasts are the sleek sportsters, leaving models such as the SCRs very much in the backwater of present buying priorities. Therefore, although they share the excellent basics of the other wide-case singles, the Street Scramblers don't command the same attention, and therefore only rate a couple of stars.

Mark 3 1968-74
When the 250 and 350 Mark 3s were introduced mid-way through 1968 they were in effect offered in either valve spring or Mark 3D (Desmo) form. For the first time in motorcycling history the customer of a production roadster was able to choose between the conventional valve spring or theoretically superior Desmodromic system.

And engines apart these first wide-case Mark 3 and Desmo models were virtually the same machines; even the engine differences between them were minor, apart from the very special cylinder heads of the Desmos. The only thing which obviously distinguished one from the other, unless a really close-up inspec-

Some 1974 Mark 3's, like this 450, were equipped with more comfortable upright bars.

44

tion took place, was the finish. The Mark 3 was painted a bright Italian racing red, which extended to the tank, toolboxes, fork yokes, top spring covers, frame stand, chainguard and rear light housing. The Desmo had a more restrained black frame, with the toolboxes and tank in a deep metallic crimson. Slightly less obvious were the "D" transfers on the side panels of the Desmo and its use of chrome plate on the headlamp shell, mudguards and tank sides, in place of the Mark 3s silver paint.

The press, then and now, couldn't really agree whether they fully approved or not. Dave Minton, testing a 450 Mark 3 in 1970 for *Motorcyclist Illustrated*, commented: "First impressions make the deepest ones, others following merely serve to push the first ones deeper. I had my first ride on a Ducati many years ago; the instant I rode away from the kerbside I knew it was a classic. Possibly there were details I disliked, but I can't remember now, for it is unimportant, the basic motorcycle was good. Each ride since then on progressively newer models have proved it to be a better motorcycle than its predecessor, but at the same time retaining everything that made the older model such a good machine. So it is

The 1968 350 "Desmo" engine. The photograph shows to full advantage the "wide-case" rear engine mountings and the 29 mm Dell'Orto SS1 carburettor (the latter was only used on 1968 models).

6/8 A brochure illustration showing a 1970/71 model 450 Mark 3D ("Desmo").

45

with these (wide-case) machines. However they may have improved over the older bikes, they are unmistakably Ducati."

Richard Simpson writing for *Classic Bike* had this to say of a 1968 250 Mark 3D he tested in the March 1987 issue: "It has poor suspension and the riding position is excruciatingly painful. The electrics are pathetic, the engine is difficult to work on and the styling is gimmicky enough to make a Japanese designer blush."

The point of all this is to show that a Ducati single, like the Mark 3, can either be brilliant or awful, depending on what *you* want out of it.

But even the recent *Classic Bike* test praised the "smooth and fast" engine and incredible handling.

Besides the frame, it was in the engine department that the major changes (read improvements!) occurred. The head design of the Mark 3 followed that of the super sporty Mach 1 (as did the carburettor). Combined with this was a general strengthening up of the bottom end, which had, on the narrow-case models, been a constant source of problems. An important alteration, for the road-going Ducati owner, was the complete redesign of the kickstarter mechanism –

always a weak point on the earlier models.

The big-end had also proved fragile, unless the machine was maintained and ridden by an experienced rider. Here it was vital on the older models to carry out regular oil changes and not allow the engine to plonk at low revs in a high gear. Even so the big-end bearing was often found wanting. With the new engine the con-rod and big-end were beefed up and the wet sump lubrication capacity increased from $3\frac{3}{4}$ to $5\frac{1}{2}$ pints. In addition larger main bearings were specified. There were also a host of more minor changes, including alterations to the gearbox and selector box.

Electrics, although still 6-volt, were uprated from 60 to 80 watts, and a larger-capacity 13-amp/hour battery installed.

For the 1969 season (and obviously from the very outset of 450 production) the Mark 3s featured a "slashed end" cone silencer, a square slide (but still 29 mm) VHB Dell'Orto carburettor and a single rather than twin filler caps for the fuel tank.

Events were to show that even with the revised lubrication and big-end, failures were still occurring. In an attempt to rectify this the big-end diameter (on the 250 and 350 models)

The 1972 350 Desmo "Silver Shotgun". Together with similar "valve spring" Mark 3 Special, this model introduced better front end (35 mm

Marzocchis and double-sided Grimeca front stopper).

Final "Desmo" model, like this 350, was an attractive bike, finished in orange-yellow and black. Note Brembo hydraulic disc at front.

was increased on three separate occasions, the last being to a 32 mm crankpin in 1974, which was also to be the final year of production.

Before this, in 1971, there were several cosmetic changes, which led to the most sporting Mark 3 Special (and the externally identical "Silver Shotgun" Desmo). Finished in a metal flake silver these continued, together with the Mark 3 tourer, until the end of 1972. The sportster had introduced the much more efficient double-sided Grimeca 180 mm drum front brake and stronger 35 mm Marzocchi front forks.

As a point of interest, very few of the 1971-72 bikes reached Britain (or for that matter North America), because both importers were in dispute with the Bologna factory over prices, and the vast majority of models imported were from the Spanish Mototrans factory – 24 Hours for Britain, 250 Road for the States.

1973 saw the arrival of the definitive Ducati overhead cam singles, the blue and gold Mark 3, the yellow café racer-styled Desmos and revised SCR Street Scramblers.

Perhaps the most noteworthy feature (not specified for the SCRs) was electronic ignition

The author with friend Leslie Boustead's very nice 1974 250 "Desmo Disc", at Cadwell Park, 1988.

47

Nearside view of the same machine.

– setting Ducati very much at the forefront of technology.

Although production ceased in late 1974, Ducati singles were still available, at least in Britain, until early 1976. This was due to importers Coburn and Hughes buying up every single they could lay their hands on from the factory. This in turn led to a real mish-mash of

The 248 cc (74 × 57.8 mm) Desmo engine. Note the folding rear-set brake pedal and footrest.

models, including 239 cc French market tax dodgers, 350 Mark 3s with Spanish Mototrans engines, and even Spanish made 250 SCRs and a small batch of the final 450 SCR – which C & H marketed as "Mark 4s". All very confusing then and now!

What to look for

Most of the wide-case Ducatis to be found in Britain are the ones imported from November 1973 (the date when Coburn and Hughes became importers in place of Vic Camp) until their final demise just over a year later (a total of around 2,500 Mark 3 Desmos and SCRs were brought in over this short time). When buying a 250 it is always worth checking to see if yours is one of the French market models.

The difference in riding the 250 (or 239), 350 or 450 is quite marked, even though the models are the same physical size.

In my opinion, the nicest engine is the 250 (239), it's smooth, economical and quite fast – a good one in standard roadster trim should always manage a genuine 85 mph. The 350 should be around 5 mph quicker, but beware the Spanish-engined Mark 3s – they are usually slower and vibrate quite horribly.

The 450 also vibrates, but has considerably more torque and will usually manage around 95 mph in Mark 3 guise.

Although the Mark 3 handles extremely well, its riding position is not always what one would want. Most of the later (blue and gold) Mark 3s imported into Britain came with clip-ons, but with the footrest position unchanged for the fitment of touring handlebars and a sit-up-and-beg riding position. The usual remedy is to fit the rear sets from the Desmo model. This entails the following: solid and folding footrests, folding (to clear the kickstarter) brake pedal, rear set gearchange pedal, linkage shaft kit, and finally the small arm which is fitted to the selector box.

With the aforementioned problem resolved, the Mark 3 (together with the drum-brake version of the Desmo) is without doubt the finest handling of all the production Ducati singles.

A particular point to watch on the 73/74 Mark 3s is the front mudguard. This is prone to rotting around the middle portion next to the stays. The other weaknesses are discussed at the end of the chapter, as they are also applicable to the Desmo (and SCR) models.

Star rating: Three full stars
Although not as popular as their Desmo brothers, the Mark 3s are nonetheless in the "worth finding" category and are likely to increase steadily in value. They are also much easier to find than the Desmos because lots more were manufactured.

Desmo 1968-74
It was not until 1973 that the Desmo was styled differently enough to its valve spring brothers to be noticed visually as another motorcycle.

But, of course, the *really* significant difference was hidden out of sight in the cylinder head. Cleverly, designer Ing. Taglioni utilized the conventional ohc engine and simply fitted a new cylinder head. Even then many items were from the "standard" unit. The main components such as the camshaft, rockers, valve guides and valves were where the changes came.

The actual design of the desmodromic

system for mechanical valve opening and closing was very similar to the one that Taglioni had devised for his early racing machines. The main difference was that the roadsters' valve closing was assisted by springs, unlike the racers, which had none at all. However, the springs employed were very much lighter than those on non-Desmo models; in fact, they were the standard items fitted to the earlier 125/160 models. Compared with the Mark 3 and SCR, the Desmos had *ten* times less valve seat pressure! – which is a benefit of the system that is usually overlooked.

On the 1968-70 models, except for the tiny "D" badge on the side panels and Desmo cam end cover on the nearside of the cylinder head just above the spark plug, the observer was almost in the dark – only its owner knew! Just why Ducati didn't go the full hog and clearly define the Mark 3 and Desmo with totally different styling and character has always been

Close-up of 1973-74 model Desmo's front wheel and disc brake assembly. Unlike the drum brake version, this had 35 mm Ceriani forks and external speedometer drive gearbox.

lost on me. When they did, from 1973 onwards, it was almost too late, in any case the majority of Mark 3s still retained clip-ons.

In performance there was never really much to separate the Mark 3 and Desmos either – even though the latter had a marginally higher top-end speed and was noticeably smoother in its power delivery.

The pre-1971 Desmos suffered like the Mark 3 with clip-ons from a poor riding position. However, with the introduction of the Silver Shotgun this was solved.

Strangely the fitting of a hydraulically operated Brembo disc brake at the front on the 1973/74 models (a drum brake was still available) allied to Ceriani forks did not improve the handling – if anything it actually made things sightly less satisfactory – due to the over-stiffness of the 35 mm Ceriani forks. These were purpose-built and not cut-down V-twin components.

The Silver Shotgun and, of course, the 1973-74 Desmo were ideally suited to sports machine racing, being equipped with all the goodies – except competition tyres – to go racing straight-out-of-the-crate!

And unlike the earlier Desmos and the Mark 3s, the café racer-styled Desmos were highly acclaimed by the world's press: "It's a pure sports machine, for enthusiasts only," claimed *Motorcycle Mechanics.* "I've been seduced," cried *Bike.* "What we mean by a good old-fashioned single," said *Motorcycle Sport,* and "taken as purely sporting motorcycles, no other small machine holds a candle to the Ducati singles for sheer road, or clubman's performance," wrote *Motorcyclist Illustrated Road Test Annual.*

Yes, judged purely from its handling, road holding, engine unit, braking or power-to-weight ratio the Desmo singles were hard to match. However, no motorcycle, certainly not an Italian one is perfect . . .

Star rating: Four solid stars
If it wasn't for a number of failings (see summary) I would be sorely tempted to award the final yellow Desmos a full five-star rating. But common sense must eventually rule over the heart. Even so you can easily fall in love, as I did with my own 350 Desmo back in 1974. But rose-tinted glasses haven't over-ruled my final judgement.

Summary
Before considering *any* Ducati singles you must remember one golden rule – these motorcycles are not suitable as a practical everyday means of transport. If you take no notice of this warning I can guarantee your time together will be frustrating to say the least. Owned by someone purely as a vehicle of pleasure you could well join the lengthy list of hardened Ducati freaks who realize the shortcomings and love the rest. However, no motorcycle is perfect and the Ducati single, even in its later, more reliable form, has a list of potential problems.

Except for the big-end problems already mentioned, instrumentation and electrics were the weakest points. Both the speedometer and tacho (where fitted) were largely undamped and not only inaccurate but suffered wildly swinging needles!

Daylight riding on Ducati singles is fun, but the lighting by today's standards is a disaster. Many owners have improved things in this direction by opting for a 12-volt conversion.

Generally, except for the need to constantly regrease the phosphor bronze swinging arm bushes, the chassis is trouble-free. It's worth nothing that the 24 steel balls in each of the two steering head races also require occasionally to be repacked with fresh grease, as do the wheel bearings.

The general level of finish, as regards the paintwork and chrome, left a lot to be desired, and as a consequence of this all Ducati singles need a garage *and* someone who likes cleaning and polishing the mass of alloy and chrome. A machine not given this attention will deteriorate rapidly and then demand a huge amount of time, effort *and* money to restore it to anything like showroom condition.

The late Mark 3s and Desmos had electronic (pointless) ignition, either Ducati Electronica (not the same company) or Motoplat. The latter system was unfortunately mainly fitted on 450s. This was a bad move, as instead of producing a nice healthy blue spark, all the Motoplat system could dish out was a feeble yellow affair. With luck all the Motoplat systems have already been junked either under warranty or by some other means years

50

ago.

The rest (over 90 per cent) of the 1973-74 singles had the Ducati system. This is fine while it is working, but there is a problem. If the pulse coil on the stator plate fails (reading 40 instead of 400 ohms) the only recourse is to fit contact breakers. This demands a new HT coil, advance and retard unit, a points back-plate assembly and a 3-pole ignition switch (replacing the original 4-pole item). Luckily the alternator is left in place (with its now defunct electronic ignition pulse coil), which keeps the cost down. Another alternative is to fit the British-made Lucas Rita system.

Besides the dreaded big-end, another potential problem with the engine is the use of pattern parts. On no account be tempted to use either a pattern con-rod (which includes the big-end) or a cast piston for racing or high-speed road work. Although much cheaper, the cost of an engine blow-up and/or accident is just not worth the risk.

Each Ducati single engine was originally assembled by hand, therefore it is individually shimmed. When stripping the motor make sure every shim remains in its correct location. Re-shimming an engine is a time-consuming and costly exercise.

Spares are still relatively easy to find, except for certain cycle parts.

Recently, Ducati singles, and in particular the sports models, have risen drastically in price, the most sought after being the Desmos with disc front brake. One of these in completely original and immaculate condition can now cost a small fortune. For a long time the Mark 3 lagged behind, but even these too are rising. In my opinion it is better (and cheaper) to pay a top price for the right bike rather than attempt to save a small sum, and then find out later than you need to spend a fortune.

Chapter 7

750 GT and Sport

★ ★ ★	750 GT 1971-74
★ ★ ★ ★	750 Sport 1972-74

History

The first Ducati V-twin was the 750 GT, the prototype of which made its bow in 1970, with the production version appearing a year later. Except for racers, Ducati had always concentrated on singles, that was until the mid-1960s, when chief designer Taglioni created a massive 1,200 V-four push-rod design for the American importers as a police bike. This never left the prototype stage. Neither did various parallel twins manufactured between 1965 and 1967 in 500 and 800 cc engine sizes.

Then came a management shake-up in 1969, which saw Arnoldo Milvio and Fredmano Spairani take over at the head of Ducati Meccanica. Under these two men the factory entered the new decade committed to manufacturing a brand new 750 – a 90-degree V-twin Superbike.

Work began almost immediately, and by early 1970 the initial design was finished and ready to be built. By mid-July that same year, the first prototype engine was running on the test bed. And amazingly two short months later, in September, a complete bike was shown to members of the Italian press!

That first model, although sporting a massive drum brake at the front, was to remain remarkably similar to the first production examples that appeared in mid-1971.

With a capacity of 748 cc (80 × 74 mm) each cylinder, like the singles, had its own bevel-driven overhead camshaft – but coil valve springs were used in place of the traditional hairpins. And on these early vees no Desmo variant was offered.

Pressed-together flywheels contained the two con-rods side by side. This allowed the rear cylinder and head to be slightly offset and placed the exhaust port in the cooling airstream. The crankshaft and gearbox were housed in cast aluminium crankcases, which also served as the oil reservoir for both. And the wet clutch operated a five-speed box.

All this was very, very similar (except the crankshaft of course!), to the long-running single line. It is also an answer to why development was so rapid – Taglioni and his team were treading a familiar path.

At first sight the new 750 GT presented observers with an obvious contradiction; on one hand the engine had a decidedly sporting flair, but the running gear appeared to have been conceived as something more suitable for a touring machine.

In fact Taglioni had built the machine around the engine. The 90-degree vee layout, adopted in the interest of not only peak efficiency but ideal balance, and thus virtually nil vibration, had the disadvantage of an over-long 61-in. wheelbase, and an over-high rear cylinder. In spite of these seeming handicaps, the Ducati engineers nonetheless came up with a bike which offered a comparable seat height and weighed in at a surprisingly low 409 lb (dry).

Early 750 GTs – in 1971 and 1972 – looked like this: metalflake tank and side panels, Lockheed front disc and Amal Concentric carburettors.

Then in 1972 came the 750 Sport – with minimal tuning and a new set of clothes it was destined to become one of Ducati's most popular models.

750 GT 1971-74

Comparison was obviously made with other, earlier V-twins, notably those from Vincent and Harley-Davidson. Like both these, the Ducati roused passions which lesser machines could not match. The comparison with the other famous vees is perhaps to be expected. But, although the Ducati's engine, like the Vincent, was mounted longitudinally in the frame, it was tilted considerably further forward, with the front pot not quite horizontal and the rear just as nearly vertical. The angle between the cylinders was at 90 degrees, much wider than the Vincent's 50 degrees, and for that matter the very similar Harley. But whatever one might say, in practice the Ducati was not only considerably smoother but also handled considerably better, even with its long wheelbase.

And as *Motorcycle Sport* so accurately put it, the Ducati 750 was: "A beautifully balanced machine . . . plus snags." *MCS* didn't like the electrics, particularly the "Micky Mouse"

Aprilia switchgear, the 45/40-watt headlight from the same source and the less than satisfactory paint finish. For example, on the machine they tested, "All the cylinder head nuts were unplated and, not surprisingly, rusty." Also the paint and chrome were not of the level expected for the price. They summed it up thus: "Here is a bike with a couple of faults

The first few 750 GT engines had this type of primary drive cover without the small inspection cover for clutch maintenance. Ignore the massive 42 mm Dell'Ortos and high level pipes of this "racerised" version.

53

that we, frankly, do not expect on a machine of this calibre."

But *Motorcycle Sport* went on to say: "No matter how many faults can be found with the bike it is impossible not to keep coming back to that magnificent engine. The power, and the manners, were outstanding. At 5,000 rpm it would be doing 70 mph and, although the noisy exhaust made it sound busier than would normally have been expected, it still managed to feel relatively unhurried."

MCS was also impressed with the gearbox, handling, suspension, economy, lazy power and the flexibility of that engine. They summed up the test with the following statement:

"We feel very little extra effort would be required to make the Big Duke the first choice of a great many riders."

There was also a "second opinion" (carried out by MRW – otherwise Mark Ramsey Wigan – who in many ways got nearer to the truth than the main tester) saying that: "ridden at 6/10 or more and you will adore it; drop the ante to 4-5/10, and it will irritate you in the way that only a well-loved member of the family can do." MRW also "forecast" (correctly) "that the Ducati will gain a following to shame the Vincent Owner's Club. He later became an enthusiast for the marque, owning, amongst other models, a Mach 1 racer and 750

For 1973 and most of 1974, the 750 GT came with a Scarab front disc, Dell'Orto carburettors and direction indicators. The last few made, at the end of 1974, had central axle forks, Brembo disc brakes and square black plastic CEV switches.

and 900 SS V-twins.

What to look for

Early models (1971 and 1972) had less than perfect glass-fibre tanks and side panels – plus Amal concentric carburettors, Lockheed front disc brake and chromed wire headlamp brackets. For 1973 the GT was given a steel tank and panels, 30 mm Dell'Orto carburettors with accelerator pumps and a Scarab front disc brake. There were new painted headlamp holders. In addition an electric start option was offered, at extra cost. 1974 saw painted mudguards – previously these had been in stainless steel. And finally the last batch constructed towards the end of that year saw the model brought into line with the new 860 with a Brembo disc, central axle forks and chrome-plated wheel rims, square black CEV switches, high touring bars (previously all European GTs had had narrow, flat ones), a large, square

rear light and other minor details. The electric start model came with a larger battery.

Except for its poor finish, the GT (together with the 750 Sport) has proved the most reliable of all the bevel-driven twins in service. By and large the 750s were free of the big-end and gearbox problems of the larger, later vees.

A problem for owners, and potential ones, of the 750 GT (and Sport) is the Scarab braking equipment. This is to be found on models manufactured from the beginning of 1973 through to September 1974. Scarab went out of business around 1977, and certain spares are simply no longer available, notably seal kits.

Rear brake hubs have been known to suffer cracking and the electric starter (which would usually only start the motor when hot) was almost always dumped, the owner preferring to rely on the kickstarter. On this subject *never* attempt to start the bike by this means whilst astride it – otherwise you will suffer a black

Some 1974 models were fitted with an electric starter – it proved unpopular.

55

Details of the Scarab disc and caliper. Spares are now a problem as Scarab went out of business in the late 1970s.

This view gives an indication of just how narrow the 750 GT 90-degree V-twin really was.

The control layout of the 1974 750 GT. Bikes came with Smiths or Veglia instruments. The mirror is non-standard, but useful.

and blue shin!

Star rating: Three firm stars
One of Ducati's best. Middle of the road rating is down to its rather conservative styling rather than anything else. Mechanically and riding wise it's got a lot going for it.

750 Sport 1972-74
To my mind, and I'm sure many others, the Sport, with its curving lines, is how designer Taglioni really saw his creation. "A slim, rakish greyhound in yellow and black, no extraneous indicators, instruments, seats or clutter such as air filters, the usual accidental coincidence of some sort of front lamp and rear lamp tacked on, and the centre-stand tucked away, way up inside the megaphones." So said MRW in the April, 1974 issue of *Motorcycle Sport*.

Bruce Ferretti of the American journal *Motorcycle World* that same year had this to say of the Ducati Sport: "When, and if, you finally get one the wait will have been worth it. You'll have the closest thing yet to the ultimate production sport motorcycle in the world." This is even though, like the men from *Motorcycle Sport*, Ferretti didn't close his eyes to such letdowns as "peeling, crooked decals, so-so glassfibre, no rear view mirror and a cramped riding position."

What really made the Sport (and to a lesser degree the GT) stand out from the crowd was the simple fact that it was the work of a single

1973-early 1974, 750 Sport — the next best thing to one of the Imola Replica 750 SS "Desmos".

man, rather than an endless committee of product planners. At the time, the Japanese might have made machines which did everything to a set standard, but in doing so failed to set any emotions into action.

Compared to these pleasant but soul-less bikes, the 750 Sport was raw *and* real – *and* fun. Loved and admired as it was, the 750 Sport was only ever made in small numbers (even compared to the GT) and was therefore always in short supply. This was a great pity as it was much more successful as a sportster than the GT could have ever been as a tourer.

Things which stood out like a sore thumb on the GT just didn't matter on the café racer Sport. Even the silencer looked right on the Sport and in contrast to the "noisy" mark awarded to the same items on the GT, *Motorcycle World* had this to say of the Conti system on their test Sport: "The sound is a deep, mellow, powerful sound, loud but not irritating. It sounds like a Harley *should* sound but without the hesitant, unbalanced 'rumpty rump' of the Harley V-twin. The mufflers are a work of art, balanced, symmetrical with substantial ground and cornering clearance, seamless construction and perfect chrome."

But what really sold the Sport was its looks

– one of the most lovely of all Ducati's production motorcycles. Also in many ways it was easier to live with than the GT. For a start it made no pretension of being anything other than a pure sporting machine. The kickstarter was easy to operate (unlike the GT) and its clip-ons and rear sets suited the Ducati image fully. The single seat even had a handy lockable compartment – much more practical than the zipped affair on the Desmo Super Sport.

A late 1974 750 Sport. This had central axle forks, Brembo disc, square black CEV switches and extended clip-ons. Very few were made.

What to look for

Contrary to common belief the Sport did not have higher-lift cams – only forged high-compression slipper pistons and larger 32 mm Dell'Orto pumper carburettors to set it aside performance-wise from its GT brother.

Even so it was suprisingly fast and only a few miles slower than the hand-built 750 SS Desmo (and don't forget this had massive 40 mm carburettors!).

There were very few changes to the Sport during its three-year life. The first few had a different paint job to the majority which followed – and an optional fairing (similar, but not the same as the SS-type). Then in 1974 the previous black for the engine outer covers and bevel tubes was left polished, or chromed (bevel tubes).

Like the GT the final few Sports had the square CEV switches, plus other smaller changes, including new clip-ons, which were extended forward slightly from the fork stanchion.

As might reasonably be expected, the Sports' only real fault was its lack of comfort, but if the journey had a few curves in it, one's mind was taken off it!

Star rating: A well earned four

The 750 Sport was one of those rare bikes when Ducati actually got things right. It also acts as a reminder that, however hard they might try, Ducati's real forté is sports bikes – and this is one of their finest. If it wasn't for the 750 Super Sport I would have awarded this machine the full five-star treatment. As if to confirm that even Ducati knew the Sport was well thought of it came up with a new model – essentially a stripped-down Paso – for the 1988 season.

Chapter 8

SS and S2

★ ★ ★ ★ ★	**750 SS 1973-74**
★ ★ ★ ★	**900 SS 1975-80**
★ ★ ★ ★	**750 SS 1975-77**
★ ★ ★	**900 SS 1981-82**
★ ★	**900 S2 1983-84**
★ ★ ★	**1000 S2 1985**

History

The story of the SS saga began with the inaugural Imola 200 for Formula 750 machines, held in April 1972. The race was billed as the Daytona of Europe, and attracted not only a good deal of publicity but also a top-line entry.

At the time Ducati were experiencing problems in marketing the new 750 GT V-twin which they had introduced the previous year, and which, although basically an excellent motorcycle, was suffering from being both rather expensive and unconventional.

The Bologna company's directors had already made one stab at road racing with a V-twin, but this machine, a 500 cc, was for Grand Prix racing, and therefore had done little to promote the roadster – if for no other reason than it was no match for the dominant MV Agustas.

So it was decided to enter a 750, based around the production bike, as not only would this be more readily indentifiable with the roadster, but less costly too.

Ing. Taglioni and his team were therefore authorized to proceed with the development of *ten* machines. Their first target had been Daytona itself, but the American organizers displayed strict rules regarding eligibility. They demanded that a minimum of 200 should be made available to the public, and that the race winner had to be auctioned off after the race – so Ducati declined to take part.

Imola they felt was different, somehow, even though the rule stating "200 examples must have, or be intended, to be made," didn't matter so much – this was Italy, not North America. In any case Imola was only a few kilometres down the *autostrada* from the Ducati factory.

What seemed less simple was the opposition ranged against the Bologna team. Included were the likes of World Champion Phil Read; the previous year's Ontario winner, John Cooper; British short-circuit star Ray Pickrell, who had recently shared overall victory in the Anglo-American match race series with Cal Rayborn; Ron Grant on a factory Suzuki; future World Champion Walter Villa and many, many more. Even the legendary Giacomo Agostini was entered on a 750 cc MV Agusta! And besides machines from Ducati, Suzuki and MV there were works bikes from Norton, Moto Guzzi, BSA, Triumph and Honda, plus some semi-works entries from Laverda and BMW. In all a total of 21 works and semi-works bikes representing nine factories lined up for the start.

As the flag fell Agostini and the lone MV streaked into the lead, with Smart and Spaggiari on the leading two Ducatis right behind. But soon first Smart and then Spaggiari overtook the MV rider, never to be headed again, to score one of the most sensational and unexpected wins in recent racing history. This overwhelming victory ensured Ducati a vast amount of post-race press

A 1974 "round-case" 750 SS "Desmo" in action on a wet Brands Hatch circuit: the rider is Charlie Sanby. The machine is one of only 24 "officially" imported into Britain.

coverage, and almost overnight everyone sat up and noticed that Ducati had a real Superbike to offer.

Fired up with enthusiasm, possibly worried by the thought of the "200 bike" rule, the firm's bosses promised that a production 750 Desmo replica of the Imola winner would follow shortly. However, in typical Italian fashion

Several 750 SS machines had high-level pipes fitted in an attempt to improve ground clearance problems. The factory also listed a performance kit, including oil cooler, cams and pipes.

it wasn't until well into 1973 that the first prototype of the production bike finally appeared.

As a whole, the works racers Ducati had constructed for the 1972 Imola race were surprisingly standard – they used standard frames (with even the centre-stand lugs left on!) and suspension. The only real changes were the triple Lockheed disc brakes and a few engine components such as con-rods, higher-compression pistons, Desmo heads, twin-plug total loss ignition, massive 40 mm Dell'Orto pumper carburettors and an oil-cooler. Cosmetically they featured the curvaceous glass-fibre fuel tank with clear strip petrol gauge and single bum-stop saddle, both of which would appear on the production version.

The 1973 Imola racer deviated considerably from the 750 GT which had formed the basis of the 1972 winner. The frame was shortened and provided a choice of three rear wheel spindle locations for alternative wheelbase lengths. Central axle Marzocchi forks replaced the former leading axle variety and brakes were now Scarab (although Lockheed was re-

60

tained at the rear). The engine was completely revamped with new bore and stroke measurements, the bore size later being used for the larger production "860" engine. Even the Desmo heads were revised, with the valve angle altered to 60 degrees and higher-lift camshafts. There was also a dry clutch.

The 1973 bike was lighter, faster and more compact, but *didn't* handle as well. A cure was found to prevent high-speed weaving by combining the type of caliper clamps used on the leading axle forks with the central axle Marzocchis. This geometry solved the problem and was incorporated into the main batch of production 750 SS models sold.

750 SS 1973-74

When the definitive production version of the 750 SS finally appeared, after another pre-production outing at the 1973 Milan Show, it,

like the few pre-production examples built in the summer of 1973, did not get the short-stroke engine or the more compact chassis. The engine and chassis were in fact based closely on the 1972 Imola racer, and for that matter the production GT and Sport, but with the front forks and brakes from the 1973 machine. The engine was, and remains, very special in terms of Ducati production.

Ing. Taglioni, assisted by right-hand man Franco Farne, personally supervised the construction of each 750 SS engine. For example, a special computer-operated cutting tool was used to machine the con-rods individually from a solid billet of specially selected material. It took over one hour to manufacture each rod, which was then built up with its mate into the crankshaft. These rods were claimed to be identical to those used in the 1972 750 racer and in terms of technology were

The 1975 750 SS — but now with 900 SS-type "square-case" engine casings.

61

the best available at the time. Although not entirely solving Ducati's infamous big-end problems, they were much more reliable (as indeed were the 750s as a whole) than the larger engines which followed. I personally have never known one of these special rods to break. The cylinder heads had a less radical camlift than the racer, there were seamless Conti silencers and the same giant 40 mm Dell'Ortos from the track bike. In 1974 it was also the *only* production motorcycle to sport triple disc brakes as standard equipment.

Some of the 1973 pre-production 750 SS models featured black outer engine casings and leading axle forks, but every 1974 model 750 SS had polished engine casings and central axle forks. Another difference was that the front mudguard was bolted to the forks, rather than being attached with Jubilee clips as the first few bikes were.

For anyone wanting to go racing with their

750 SS, a whole host of "extras" were available. These included fiercer-lift Imola cams, a set of high-level pipes and unrestricted "competition use only" open megaphones, a full fairing and a range of sprockets and jets, plus an oil-cooler.

With the announcement of the 750 SS the world's press had a field day and Ducati benefitted from a succession of rave reviews . . . here's just a sample: *Cycle,* June 1974: "And then there is the Ducati Super Sport, a bike that stands at the farthest reaches of the sporting world – the definitive factory-built café racer." In Britain the 1974 issue of *Motor Cyclist Illustrated Road Test Annual* had this to say: "I swear by whichever owners' club you hold dearest, and without fear of rational contradiction, that the 750 Desmo Ducati is the finest sports motorcycle to have yet seen the light of day."

Heady stuff, but even testers hardened to

The 1976 900 SS entered by Mick Walker
Motorcycles in the Isle of Man TT that year. It was
standard except for Girling rear shocks.

62

giving adverse criticism rather than praise admitted that they *loved* their time with the Desmo Duke. All this was just reward for the team who had created this mechanical masterpiece. Unfortunately the masterpiece was dressed in tatters. This statement does not refer to its style but to the poor level of finish on many ancillary parts.

The glass-fibre ware in particular left a lot to be desired. Even the enthusiastic *Cycle* tester had this to say: "Rust is intruding through the surface of the frame's rather shoddy paint (that doesn't match the rather shoddy paint on the tank, seat or fender). The fuse box is mounted upside down and is open to the punishment of lousy weather. A hole has been crudely filed in the rear inner-fender to make room for the rear brake line. And there's an honest-to-God Italian fly moulded into the fibre glass fuel tank."

And unlike other Superbikes of the era it did not boast an abundance of cylinders, electric starter, air cleaners, flashing indicators, rows of idiot lights – there wasn't even provision for a female companion! The 750 SS was just raw motorcycling with a pure heart. *Cycle* again: "What time the Italians of the Ducati factory haven't spent on the fibre glass they have positively lavished on the engine." Matching that engine was its production racing cornering ability, which complemented the Desmo powerplant perfectly.

Unlike many other racers, the 750 SS could run effectively at lower engine speeds, making use of the tremendous torque available. Even so, it was happiest out on the race circuit, or being used to the full on sparsely populated roads. Sure, it couldn't be labelled comfortable in the same way as a BMW or even a Guzzi, but it did have a near perfect riding stance – for fast road work or racing use. This was totally uncompromising and aimed both at giving

The black and gold 900 SS was introduced in 1978: it featured several changes including cast alloy wheels, Darmah-type bottom end, with Bosch ignition, and dual-seat.

and extracting the last ounce of performance from the big twin.

It is debatable if the desmodromic valve operation actually assisted in making the 750 SS engine smoother than its valve spring brothers – more likely the flowing power delivery can be attributed more to the extra attention lavished by the men who built it.

Like the GT and Sport, the SS, when compared to other manufacturers' V-twins, was definitely blessed with less vibration. This was in no small part due to the theoretically perfect 90-degree layout. The "L" shape, as Ing. Taglioni called it, had one disadvantage – an overlong wheelbase. But on the SS this only really made itself apparent on slow corners. In contrast to the typical Japanese Superbike of the era the suspension on the Ducati was *hard*. Not firm, or stiffly damped, but hard and uncompromising, made for dealing with high-speed work and very little else.

Maximum speed and acceleration are not so easily defined. Possibly because of its hand-built nature each 750 SS seemed different as regards engine performance (even Paul Smart noticed this with the racers). Another thing was that performance was deceptively rapid. Maximum speed ranged from 122 mph by *Motor Cyclist Illustrated* up to 135 mph by the respected German publication *Das Motorrad*. Somehow the almost lazy engine note made you *think* you were travelling more slowly than you actually were.

Mark Wigan, writing about his own 750 SS in the May 1976 issue of *Motorcycle Sport*, commented: "The entire picture changes within 15 seconds of starting to drive (ride!) the SS. It is simply magical in the manner in which it reaches out for the next piece of road, and then promptly demolishes it. The spread of torque makes this long and lazy-steering motorcycle positively enjoyable to ride with its ability to accelerate instantly in any gear and any speed."

Ducati never officially released power figures, but I would estimate somewhere between 62-65 bhp. What really made the machine quick between two given points was not outright power but a combination of low weight, a broad power band, superb handling and efficient brakes – put all these factors together and you have the reason why the 750 SS was such a formidable machine on road or track.

Unlike the GT and Sport, the SS was equipped with an 18-in. front wheel rim. This had the disadvantage of endowing the sportster with *less* ground clearance, so it was possible to touch down both the kickstart and centre stand. For racing it was important to not only remove these but also to fit the optional high-level exhaust system.

Dave Railton cranks his Chris Clarke-entered 900 SS over near the limit at the British Grand Prix, Silverstone 1982.

The gearbox and clutch were good, although, like the rest of the Ducati V-twins, there was an overheavy clutch action. Unlike the problems encountered on the larger SS models – broken gear cogs and slipping clutches – the 750 SS generally had a reliable record in these areas.

One worthwhile modification – and one which doesn't alter the appearance – is Lucas RITA electronic ignition. Not only adding reliability, it saves the owner the time-consuming job of setting up the ignition and adjusting the two sets of points.

What to look for
Because of their poor paint and chrome it is unlikely that *any* 750 SS remains in a totally unrestored and immaculate condition. Even so, because they have always been held in high regard by their owners, it is likely that the majority will be in either a nicely restored and/or mechanically healthy condition. The main problem is whether you are actually buying a *real* 750 SS. At least as many spurious

examples are in circulation as genuine ones. Before parting with your money make *absolutely* certain . . .

Be prepared to pay a substantial sum for a pukka 750 SS which is sound inside and outside – it will be worth even more soon. Finally check the capacity – several 750 SS models were converted to 900 SS engine size by increasing the bore size to 86 mm.

Star rating: Full five stars
If any Ducati V-twin deserves the full five-star treatment it is the 1973-74 round-case 750 SS. Many enthusiasts consider it the best sport bike *ever* – and I'd agree with them.

900 SS 1975-82, 750 SS (square case) 1975-77
Originally planned, like the 750 SS, as a strictly limited quantity, hand-built super sportster, the 900 SS instead became a best seller.

The Ducati management had planned their 1975 model range the previous year. This consisted of the 125 Regolarita, 350 GTL, and 860 GT, none of which followed the Ducati tradi-

1981 and the 900 SS was updated yet again with new colours (silver/blue), seat, air filters and more

restrictive Silentium silencers among other differences.

65

tion of high-performance sporting roadsters. The factory's plan also called for some 200 900 SS and 750 SS (with a ratio of 75/25 respectively) to be constructed in place of the original 750 SS model. The "new" 750 SS was to be a smaller-bore version of the 900 SS, rather than the 1974 type. Not for the first time, as history shows, the Ducati planners got it badly wrong! None of the mainstream models proved popular with the punters, with the result that it soon sold out of the SS models and was stuck with large quantities of the supposed mainstream production.

The prototype of the larger-capacity 864 cc (86 × 74.4 mm) machine had made (like its smaller brother) a race-winning début. This time the venue was the twists and turns of Montjuich Park, the Barcelona 24 Hours endurance marathon, which the Spanish pairing of Benjamin Grau and Salvador Canellas won in July 1973.

In reality the "prototype" had actually been a 750 SS bored out to 86 mm and fitted with a dry clutch and other racing goodies from the 1973 Imola race. Whereas the 900 SS, like the standard 750 SS, used production parts, including the same gearbox and clutch as the 750 GT and Sport, the larger-bore sportster shared the same 40 mm Dell'Ortos as the smaller SS.

The 900 S2 replaced the 900 SS in 1983. It proved a poor seller. Many saw it as only a shadow of the original.

But otherwise much of the engine assembly was new. There were re-profiled camshafts, Ducati Electronica electronic ignition, consisting of a sealed ignition pack within the engine and two separate transducers (identical to those fitted on the late singles) and, unlike its 860 GT stablemate, a 200-watt alternator.

But perhaps the most significant change was an outrigger bearing plate to locate the crank and cam bevel gears more precisely. This removed a weakness of the earlier design, where there had been *five* bottom bevel gears! On the new layout there were only three of these and their support was much more rigid. Another noteworthy improvement was a fully replaceable oil cartridge. This was located in the position previously occupied by the distributor, between the vee of the cylinders. The primitive washable nylon oil strainer-cum-drain plug remained in the finned sump at the base of the crankcases. New square, slab-sided, outer engine casings, inherited from the 860 GT, gave the engine a much more angular look.

Differences to the running gear included triple Brembo drilled cast iron discs, Marzocchi forks with modified caliper mounters and a new silver and blue colour scheme. The 900 SS had a blue fairing with silver stripes, a scheme which was reversed on the smaller model. Incidentally, although the square-case 750 SS was mainly intended for the home market, some of the bikes were exported, notably to Australia.

By the end of 1975 Ducati had been left in no doubt that their distributors and importers, at home and abroad, wanted the 900 SS – and not the "cooking" models. So for 1976 the SS was scheduled for mass production. The "'mass", of course, being in relation to Ducati's small overall production figures.

Suddenly the model had left the realms of the hand-built specialist production racer – and once again the management displayed their lack of understanding of what made a customer buy one of their bikes. With the rejection of the civilized models and the high demand for the raw-boned SS they should have realized – but of course they didn't! So what happened? The 1976 750 SS/900 SS were initially offered with smaller 32 mm carburettors, air filters, restrictive (and quiet!) Lafran-

66

coni seamed silencers, a larger rear light and even direction indicators! The result was such a loud noise from Ducati purists that the factory was forced to backtrack and refit the bikes with 40 mm carburettors, Conti's, and junk all the other unpopular items.

Other changes to the 1976 models were a left-hand gearchange (achieved by a cross-over shaft), which meant revised controls and new footrests with rubbers, and a smaller steel petrol tank.

All this, of course, reflected the fact, even if the customers didn't, that times were changing and manufacturers, including Ducati, were having to take note of the call from governmental departments and legislators around the world, particularly in North America and Germany, who were beginning the *anti* campaign. These markets suffered from a paranoia over lead fumes, carbohydrates, back pressure, air pressure, noise, being noticed, not being noticed – and all the rest, which were to result in the SS models becoming more and more muzzled with each passing year.

In its early days (1975-77) the 900 SS enjoyed considerable success on the race track – before the Japanese got their chassis to match the power of their engines . . . top British short-circuit rider Percy Tait track-tested a 900 SS in early 1976, and concluded that a well-set-up Ducati could: "Do very well in the Isle of Man or the Bol d'Or with its good handling, good brakes and good power range." The ex-Triumph works rider estimated top speed to "Be around the 140 mph mark." And he summed the 900 SS up "As the best ready-to-race production racer that money can buy." Quite some compliment from a rider with over twenty years of racing experience.

With sales of the 900 SS going very well the two SS models continued into 1977 unchanged, except for a new handlebar switch from CEV. At the end of the year, the 750 SS was dropped. 1978 saw the introduction of several changes. Most apparent was that the now familiar blue and silver finish had given way to a totally new black and gold colour scheme. There was a choice of either single racing saddle or dual-seat.

The wire wheels were replaced by cast alloy assemblies; this was largely due to fashion,

rather than engineering, as they were also heavier! In addition they brought problems. The first cast alloy wheels were Campagnolo, but both these and their Speedline replacements had an Achilles' heel. The six securing bolts holding the cush drive housing on the body of the rear wheel were prone to work loose and both wheels suffered hairline cracks, bad enough whilst under warranty, but even more drastic if you had to pay for this unwanted pleasure! Later Ducati fitted FPS wheels, which largely solved the problem. Another item which caused many warranty claims was broken pivots on the kickstart lever. Even today this is not an unheard of problem. Although it was more powerful than the bike it had replaced, the 900 SS was also to suffer mechanical defects which never appeared on the 750 SS. Notably big-end failure and gear problems.

Even with these faults the 900 SS still proved a popular and much sought after motorcycle. Owners loyally defended it, the press when let loose on one usually raved.

An owner writing in *Motorcycle Sport* had this to say: "And what a flag bike! When ridden for what it was designed, it is one of the very best available. At 4,000 rpm in top gear, a true 70 mph can be maintained with petrol consumption at 58 mpg."

Bike magazine got a timed 131.5 mph, which rather proved the 900 SS to be no quicker than the 750 SS, although it has to be admitted the larger engine offers better acceleration. The speed obtained probably reflects that the 900,

An S2 converted by Dave Rayner to a customer's requirements to look like a 900 SS!

67

unlike the 750, was not built with quite the same level of care. Properly screwed together and fully sorted out the 900 SS has a 140 mph *potential*. Ducati claimed 140 mph with 40 mm carburettors and Contis; and 127 mph with 32 mm carburettors, Lafranconis and air filters.

1978 also saw the improvements which had been incorporated into the newly introduced Darmah model find their way into the 900 SS production, including a totally new gear selector mechanism. This had been relocated into the left-hand side of the engine, so doing away with the cross-over shaft and linkages. Also changed were the footrests, now like the very early SS models, with no rubbers, the gearchange and brake pedals, and Bosch ignition and Nippondenso coils replaced the previous Ducati Electronica components. Likewise, a CEV headlamp took the place of the Aprilia unit, but remained at 170 mm. Finally the handlebar switchgear was now by Nippondenso – finally silencing press criticism in this area. Like the blue/silver 900 SS before it, the black and gold model continued to sell well over the next three years.

Then, for 1981, came another major up-

date. Some changes were cosmetic, some were because Ducati were having to tow the line demanded by stricter governmental controls. So there were new, much quieter, Silentium silencers, air filters, flashers and smaller 32 mm carburettors yet again. For some markets, including Britain, larger carbs and no air filters were still allowed, but everyone had the new silencers and flashing indicators. The blue/silver paint scheme, with multicoloured blue stripes, replaced the black and gold and a completely new dual-seat with compressed foam rubber completed the transformation. By now the 900 SS had lost most of its raw edges, but in the process had surrendered a certain amount of character.

In the early 1980s a deep recession hit all the motorcycle manufacturers, including Ducati. The result was that after the revised model was introduced sales fell sharply, including the 900 SS, and by the end of 1982 the last SS models were leaving the factory with a new model in the wings ready to fill the gap it would leave – or so the factory hoped.

The machine in question was the 900 S2, and the final civilization of the bevel driven

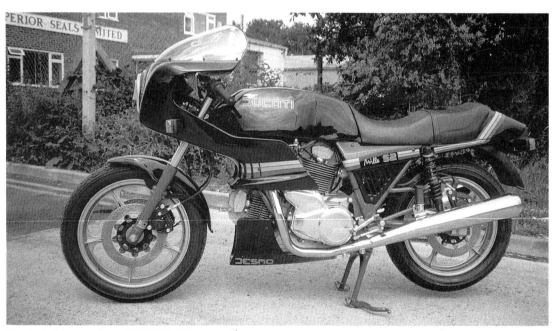

The last of the line. The 1985 1000 S2 Mille, with larger bore engine and many improvements over the 900 S2.

68

V-twin had begun . . .

What to look for
As I've already made clear, the 900 SS in its various forms is not without its faults; shot big-ends, broken gears, slipping clutches, faulty cast alloy wheels, broken kickstart levers – to name the major offenders. With all this, it is still a motorcycle which stirs real passion – and a classic of the 1970s.

As a rule, the earlier the bike the more valuable and collectable it is. This is not so much simply because it's older, more that the earlier models were what the SS series was really all about: a single-purpose, raw sportster, the nearest thing to a full-blown racer on the road in its day.

Star rating: 900 SS 1975-80 (and square-case 750 SS) four stars; 900 SS 1981-82 three stars
Unlike the 750 SS, the 900 SS (except the first few in 1975), was a standard production model within the factory's range. And as such large numbers were built so the larger SS is never going to share the rarity of the earlier Desmo sportster.

For example it is possible to see at least one or two 900 SS models advertized in the British press each week, at reasonable prices depending upon year and condition. I've occassionally seen bikes needing major surgery – a blown bottom end (big-end or gearbox), for a very low figure. An immaculate early 900 SS can cost considerably more. With a good choice of machines, take you time and make *sure* that you end up with the right bike.

Finally it is significant that the 900 SS was never eclipsed by the potentially more glamorous Mike Hailwood Replica, with many Ducati freaks preferring the original sportster to the very end of its days.

900 S2 1983-84, 1000 S2 1985
Following a legend is always difficult. *Motor Cycle News*, when testing the new 900 S2 in their 10 August, 1983, issue, had this to say on the motorcycle which had replaced the popular 900 SS: "Probably the last true Ducati is possibly the worst they've ever produced. A sad fact is that, despite turning in a respectable 130 mph, the 900 S2 has been transformed by a 'civilization' programme from the free-

revving big cat of the last decade to an animal with canine qualities. Up against the beautiful creations from the Bologna factory, the S2 is a dog." Strong words, but there were more: "Whereas the recently tested Laverda had risen to the challenge of noise restrictions with greater breathing efficiency, the Duke has simply collected its choking mufflers, huge air box and electric start like an old man collects grey hairs."

Having tested the same bike for *Motorcycle Enthusiast*, I concur *MCN's* findings. Although I didn't carry out a maximum speed or acceleration test with the machine, I still know it wasn't a patch on the earlier unrestricted 900 SS models. As if to offer proof that they were choking the engines, the silencers suffered heat-blueing areas which appeared half-way along their length. Maybe it was a combination of the air filters and restrictive silencers, but the S2 didn't seem to accelerate like earlier models, progress being ponderous by comparison. That is not to say the bike wasn't fast, for its tall gearing offered 100 mph cruising at 6,000 rpm. But quite frankly it would have performed better with a couple more teeth on the rear wheel sprocket.

What was really lacking most, compared to the 900 SS, was mid-range punch. And as the *MCN* tester revealed: "A ratio or two will have to be sacrificed to get the motor spinning, something unheard of with Ducatis a few years back." But the same journalist was much more enthusiastic about the handling, at least on fast "A" roads: "Here was the fun I had on the S2, which still handles as well as Bimota, Harris or Moto Martin. Here, where speeds can be kept constantly high, corners melted into straights as the Duke's incredible stability scoffed at lesser machines' attempts to keep up." But, as I found, you were reminded of its drawbacks just as soon as you hit slower, more bumpy going, where the overhard suspension could not cope half as well.

The 1983 S2 was offered with or without an electric start – either you had an electric button or a kickstart lever – but not both, unlike the various SS models, which only ever came with a kickstart. One definite plus for the S2 was reliability. 1983 saw the introduction of stronger cogs, which at last finally put to rest the gearbox gremlins – an added advantage is that these gears will fit into earlier engines . . .

Compared with the 130 mph obtained by *MCN*, the rival *Motor Cycle Weekly* could only record 123.94 mph. But they did make the comment: "The Duke is so long-legged it was still accelerating through the timing lights." Unlike *MCN* (and myself), Paul Carroll, who carried out the test for *MCW*, was more impressed with the S2: "I've been pleasantly surprised in my first Ducati test to find I enjoyed every moment of it. It's the kind of bike that every rider I met took an interest in, whether they were riding a Suzuki, Lambretta, Puch Maxi or Harley. My initial impression was that it wasn't as nice looking as the 900 Super Sport, but the restyled bodywork, now more like its small brother, the 600 Pantah, grows on you."

Carroll didn't like the pillion end of the seat – neither did my wife! – who complained that it was all too easy to slip backwards or forwards on the rubber foam seat moulding, thus giving a feeling of insecurity, as no grab handle was provided. The overhard rear suspension, even on the softest setting, didn't help either.

In typical Ducati fashion though, like the Pantah, there was a very neat and practical fold-up lever provided to facilitate the centre-stand operation. Another bonus of the S2 were the excellent Nippondenso instruments – the same as fitted to the Darmah and Pantah. *MCW* considered the machine's best features to be: "Good fuel consumption," and "superb handling" and its worst "restricted steering lock" and "uncomfortable pillion position."

For 1984 the S2 remained mechanically unchanged, but featured a new colour scheme. Out went the gunmetal grey and black, in came a striking combination of red chassis, with black tank, seat and fairing. The garish red, orange and yellow striping introduced on the S2 remained unchanged.

Then, in early 1985, came the final variant, the 1000 S2. Like the Mike Hailwood Replica Mille, the 1-litre S2 was much more than a simple bigger-bore job.

For a start, both the bore *and* stroke were altered – 88×80 mm – giving 973 cc. But the factory's engineers didn't stop there. They added a hydraulic clutch, a revised lubrication system with a full-flow, screw-type filter, plain bearing big-ends and substantially revised engine casings. In addition there was an improved dual-seat, new-style cast alloy wheels and brake discs, electro fuel taps, revised instrument console and belly pan – plus other more minor alterations.

The "1000" was also offered with two levels of performance, 83 and 90 bhp. The difference was a two-into-one exhaust and bellmouths for the 40 mm carburettors – in place of the Silentium silencers and air filters. The factory *claimed* 146 and 137 mph respectively, which, if accurate, made the performance version of the 1000 S2 the fastest of the whole SS/S2 family. Certainly the 1-litre S2 was a significantly better motorcycle than the small version.

Its main problem is that it was available for only a few months in 1985, before the Cagiva takeover that year. In the light of what was in reality virtually a major redesign it would appear that Ducati didn't have time to recoup their investment and that spares could be a problem in the future for those parts different to the earlier models. As is related later, Cagiva promptly pensioned off the bevel-driven twins to concentrate on the Pantah-based engines.

What to look for
Over some 2½ years of production very few S2s of either capacity were actually produced, as the company had reached a position where it found it increasingly difficult to continue trading. I feel that, of the two bikes, the larger one is much the better, but I'd worry about potential parts problems.

Star rating: 900 S2 two stars, 1000 S2 three stars
None of the S2s have the charisma of the SS models, even though they are probably more practical – and certainly more reliable – for everyday use. But how many Ducati buffs use their pride and joy as personal transport? Most are ridden on sunny days and holidays, so high-mileage reliability and practicality don't score as highly as riding fun, style or aura. And unfortunately the S2s can't match the SS models in these areas – hence the low star ratings.

Chapter 9

GT and GTS

★	860 GT 1974-75
★	860 GTS 1976
★ ★	900 GTS 1976-78

History

The Ducati V-twin craze started in 1971, following the launch of the 750 GT model. Later, in April the following year, racing versions with Desmo valve gear, piloted by Paul Smart and Bruno Spaggiari, scored an impressive 1-2 victory to scoop Europe's richest prize at the inaugural Imola 200 road race. From then on, the Ducati V-twin's reputation as a motorcycle, which combined a sweet blend of roadholding, braking and a powerful torquey engine, spread like wildfire. It also possessed a certain mystique: style, charisma, call it what you will, it was neat.

Replicas of the winning Imola machines were produced in limited quantities as the 750 SS; they were the nearest thing to an all-out legal racer and were snapped up by enthusiasts who could not only afford the high price but appreciated what they represented, an engineering victory over the cost accountant. By 1974, there were three 750 models on offer – the GT, Sport and the SS Desmo.

Then, in 1975, enter the 860 GT, a *Grand Touring* bike, one built for the masses, one that could go fast and far with both a rider and passenger in comfort. The 860 concept was a far cry from the previous raw-boned Ducatis, and was intended to open up a whole new dimension for the factory and its potential customers – well that at least was the theory . . .

860 GT

The 860s' (864 cc actually) début had come on the race circuit, at the 1973 Barcelona 24 Hours endurance race, which it had won. But this bike, a works Desmo racer, shared little in common, except its engine capacity, with the pre-production prototype that the factory displayed at the Milan Show the following November.

Called the GTI, this was a very angular-style tourer, quite unlike the Barcelona racer, and it didn't have Desmo valve gear either!

By the time the full production model appeared in the autumn of 1974 it had lost the nose-cone fairing of the show bike, sported high and wide 'bars and carried the GT prefix. The styling of the new machine not only dominated its appearance, but ultimately determined its fate.

Ducati had enlisted the services of the well-known automobile stylist Girogetto Giugiaro of the Ital design studio in Milan. However gifted Giugiaro may have been with his four-wheel creations, his efforts for Ducati can only be adjudged a disaster. But in many ways, it is not Giugiaro who should take the responsibility for this, but the Bologna factory's management, who had given him an almost impossible brief – "produce a machine which will widen our range and will mean everything to everyone."

Given this policy, is it any wonder that in the succeeding months after the launch Ducati

71

found demand lagging further and further behind production? The eventual result was that the futuristic angular styling given to the machine by Giugiaro had to be admitted by the Ducati management to be a failure and was the source of humiliation.

The original tank was a slab-side creation, whilst the equally ugly dual-seat was kicked up at the rear.

In an attempt to enable stocks to be moved in an ever overloaded storage area within the factory, a new rounded styled of tank and seat, together with narrower flatter handlebars, were conceived, this machine being sold as the GTS.

But before proceeding to the GTS, it is important to look in more detail at the 860 design, as it marked a significant staging point in the evolution of the bevel-driven V-twins.

Compared to the earlier 750s, the 860 GT incorporated a host of changes, including several internal improvements over the original design.

The larger capacity was achieved by increasing the bore size of the cylinders to 86 mm, whilst the stroke remained as before. Other differences within the engine unit included an electronic pack, courtesy of Ducati Electronica, a complete redesign of the bottom bevel support, a new oil pump (although still of the gear type) and, perhaps most noteworthy of all, a fully disposable car-type cartridge oil filter. This was mounted in the space previously occupied by the distributor in the 750s, between the two cylinders.

To fall into line with the Japanese, a left-hand gearchange was achieved by a cross-over shaft which passed through the engine to connect up with a linkage and hence to pick up with the gear selector box, which still retained its off-side location as it had done on the 750 bevel-driven V-twins – or for that matter the singles.

The Dell'Orto 32 mm pumper carburettors were the same as fitted to the 750 Sport (the 750 GT had smaller 30 mm instruments), but

A styling exercise which went wrong. Ducati commissioned top car stylist Giugiaro to design the 860 GT bodywork, but few liked it.

72

in place of the open bellmouths on the Sport, the 860 GT had more civilized air boxes with throw-away filters, connected to the carburettors by rubber hoses. Like the later 750 GTs, the 860 GT was offered with or without an electric starter. Unlike the smaller bike, owners usually chose the electric thumb method, if for no other reason than that by this time there were enough Ducati owners around to retell the tales of badly bruised shins from operating the awkwardly placed right-hand-mounted kickstart lever!

The electric start variant was marketed as the GTL in North America and the E/S in Britain. Either way, these machines all suffered from wrongly geared starter motors. Quite simply the ratio was too high – which meant that starting on the electric thumb from cold was *almost* impossible.

To cope with the extra power needed by the electric starter a larger battery was now specified. The 860s' outer engine casings were

also angular to match the angular styling lines of the Giugiaro tinware, unlike the rounded type on the 750s, but, unlike the metal work, these alloy castings were retained on succeeding models.

If one discounts the new frame with eccentric chain adjustment, and of course the Giugiaro styling cosmetics the 860 GT shared most of the running gear with the final batch of 750 GTs produced in late 1974. These late 750 components included wheels, forks, headlamp, tail-lamp, handlebar switches and silencers.

Star rating: One star
The September issue of the American magazine *Cycle World* highlighted a very good reason *why* the 860 GT ultimately failed to find customers. *CW* said: "But what, then, is the problem? It looks as though an effort has been made to get away from the sporty look, and the 860 thus appears now in a vanilla package, something that has little aesthetic appeal for us." The validity of this statement is evidenced today by the fact that very few 860 GTs remain with Giugiaro's work intact – most owners

The 860 GT used electronic ignition in place of points on 750s.

Like parallel twins of the same era the GT had eccentric chain adjusters in the swinging arm pivot.

choosing to transform their bike into something more akin to the more conventional, sporting Ducati image. This illustrates clearly just how out of tune the factory's management really was. The pity was that underneath the civilized clothes was a machine with several *technical* advantages over the model it replaced.

Whichever way you look at it all this adds up to the 860 GT coming out bottom in any list of Ducati bevel-driven V-twins and, therefore, rates a solitary single star. I can't visualize the GT *ever* being really sought after. It seems destined to remain a model for those who can't afford the real thing.

860 GTS
Next came the GTS, which was in reality a GT, but with a different tank, seat and flatter, shorter bars. In addition it came with twin front discs as standard (some later GTs also had this arrangement) and a few minor internal improvements, such as valve guides and clutch bearings. But largely the 860 GTS was born out of a necessity to move the stock of unsold GTs. Luckily for Ducati this ploy worked,

with the buying public voting with their wallets to the styling change.

Star rating: Still one star
Although it proved a better seller, the 860 GTS still wasn't *really* what the potential buyer wanted. Again press comment from the period is worth noting. *Motor Cyclist Illustrated* (November 1976) commented: "For how long can we continue to forgive Ducati for their myriad fringe transgressions just because the heart of their motorcycles is so pure." The report went on in a spirit of suggesting the public would not continue indefinitely forgiving, whatever the correct fundamentals. It was pointed out that lamentable switch gear, tricky starting, thin paint and chrome, poor lighting and a general air of ancillary part neglect was not only unacceptable it was unnecessary. In praise of the machine the test claimed that with these improved the GTS would be the equal of the best available in its class. So once again a single star is appropriate.

900 GTS
Although at first glance the 900 GTS was the

To move stocks of unsold GTs in 1976 Ducati launched the 860 GTS. Basically it was the same bike, but with a new tank, seat and instrument console. All GTs featured electric start as standard.

The 900 GTS: although still of 864 cc engine capacity, it was a definite improvement over the 860 GT/GTS. Final versions had Darmah bottom ends.

same bike, except for a pair of 900 stickers on the side panels, in truth things were somewhat different. But first, *don't* be fooled into believing what you read. Ducati had *not* added more cubic capacity, for like the 900 SS, the 900 GTS still had the same engine dimensions as the 860!

Although there were several noticeable improvements, such as stainless steel mudguards, a CEV instead of Aprilia headlamp and, on later models, even a Darmah-type bottom end, including the Bosch ignition, improved electrics and double-skinned exhaust pipes, the major updates were in things such as build quality, superior paintwork and deeper chrome. The starter motor now even started the engine from cold!

Worth mentioning at this stage are the performance figures. These included a timed maximum speed of 116 mph (rider prone in racing leathers) and a fuel consumption which averaged around 50-55 mpg, ridden *really* hard as low as 36 mpg and with a best of 77.6 mpg.

Combined with the torque, handling, braking *and* improved ancillaries, *Motor Cyclist Illustrated* were suitably impressed enough

when testing the 900 GTS to say: "Probably the finest large-capacity all-rounder in production at the present time."

But all this had come too late – the 900 GTS was obsolete the moment Ducati unveiled the Darmah.

Star rating: Two stars
Even though it was a considerable improvement over the earlier "cooking" models, the 900 GTS still does not appeal to enthusiasts and collectors of the bevel-driven V-twins in the same way as do certain other models, notably the 750s, the Mike Hailwood Replica, or the SS models.

This is not to say it should however be totally ignored. As prices of the more popular models continue to rise, the 900 GTS is worth considering, if only because or its lower price.

This was a reason why I labelled it a *Practical Classic* in the March 1988 issue of *Motorcycle Enthusiast*. The price in 1988 in Britain for a pristine example was up to two-thirds cheaper than the price of a 900 SS in similar condition. However, this final point is also the reason why it still only earns a two-star rating.

Chapter 10

Vertical Twins

★	**GTL 350, 500 1975-77**
★ ★ ★	**Sport Desmo 350, 500 1977-82**
★ ★	**GTV 350, 500 1979-83**

History

Although in the early 1960s there had been racing Ducatis with vertical twin engines, when the roadsters appeared on the market in 1975 the potential customer for a Bologna-built machine didn't associate it with the marque in the same way as the two-strokes had never really made their mark for the same reason. Yes, the British built vertical twins, and so did the Japanese, but Ducati, no, never! But they did build them and because this was so out of character was the reason, in my opinion, why they never sold them in any quantity.

At the time they were launched the Ducati management had performed another musical chairs act with the result that they were likely to get their marketing sums even more wrong than usual.

The reasoning behind the middleweight vertical twin concept was simple, at least for Ducati's new management team. The Japanese were selling lots of similar devices, so why not grab a slice of the action? This principle may work well enough in selling fridges, televisions or even tins of baked beans, but motorcycles are different, and Ducatis in particular.

The whole reason someone bought a Ducati was because it *wasn't* a Japanese-type bike. The other valid reason – had the same management team bothered to trace back in history – was that customers wanted out-and-out sports bikes from the company, not everyday tourers.

GTL 350, 500

These were the original concept motorcycles for capturing that important sector of the market in the mid-1970s – the middleweight, touring, overcam twin – the formula which had sold millions of bikes for the Japanese. Rumour has it that Ing. Taglioni didn't want anything to do with the project, but even so underneath an unexciting set of clothes, with which the GTL models were kitted out, were many things which the Ducati enthusiast could still get interested in. But these were really deep and out of sight, so the usual Ducati customer wasn't attracted and neither in the main were the "new" customers which the company expected either.

There was nothing *really* wrong mechanically with the design and this point was highlighted by a *Cycle World* test. *CW* said: "It's a nice little bike (at least by American standards!). People who don't need to leap away from the lights on the rear wheel, and who are confident enough in their judgement so as not to require instant approval from the guys at the drugstore, should find the Ducati 500 GTL very much to their liking."

Very unlike the famous ohc singles and V-twins the vertical twin featured chain-driven ohc, plain bearing big-ends and of course that engine configuration. The engine was very bulky in appearance, which on the 500 was just about acceptable, but on the 350 gave a definite impression of a poor power-to-weight ratio – *Cycle World* described them as: "shaped like a teardrop going the wrong way."

Atop the crankcases sat a equally massive set of squared alloy cylinders (cast in one) with replacable steel liners. These were painted black, which gave the impression of being cast iron. Above these sat the cylinder head casting, which featured a single camshaft, with an integral drive sprocket in the centre for the cam chain, which ran between the cylinders. The rocker arms were of a similar design to the single and V-twin type and there were two valves per cylinder. The cylinders were canted 10 degrees from the vertical, whilst the valves were angled at 60 degrees.

With the larger engine at 78×52 mm bore and stroke, and 71.8×43.2 mm for the 350 giving respective capabilities of 496.9 cc and 349.6 cc, both were severely oversquare, and this in theory offered the opportunity for considerable development and tuning.

Most vertical twins featured 360-degree cranks (with both pistons rising together); not so the Ducati design, with a 180-degree version one piston was at TDC (Top Dead Centre) the others at BDC (Bottom Dead Centre). This meant that at low/medium engine speeds vibration increased, but at higher engine speeds it was reduced. And so it proved in reality.

As if to act as confirmation the gearchange had been designed from the offset to operate on the left – just as the middleweight Japanese twins did. A definite bonus, at least compared with its V-twin brothers , was the finger-light clutch operation. And although a kickstart lever was provided there was also an electric starter as standard, with 12-volt electrics.

The 500 had twin discs at the front, the 350 single, all of 260 mm diameter. The rear brake was a 160 mm drum of the type fitted to the singles. The frame, like the recently introduced 860 GT, had eccentric alloy block for chain adjustment located in the swinging arm. Other details included chrome-plated exhaust system, with a pair of seamed Lafranconi silencers and painted mudguards. These latter components were in steel as were the side panels.

The 350 GTL made its début at the same time as the similarly styled 860 GT V-twin. It proved no more popular than the bigger bike.

77

500 GTL

BICILINDRICO   TWIN

Also offered was the 500 GTL, externally identical,
except for twin discs and "500" badging.

In an attempt to rescue disastrous sales, Ducati
asked Italjet boss Leo Taratarini to restyle and Ing
Taglioni to design a "Desmo" Sport.

What to look for

Except for very minor changes, such as improved switchgear and new headlamp brackets, the two GTL models stayed the same throughout their production life. Outside Italy very few of these models were sold. A few 500s went to North America, but no GTLs were "officially" imported into Britain.

Rating: One star

The GTLs were not popular when new, and are no more so today. In my opinion they are at the very bottom of any possible buyer's list and will remain so – if you must have one at least it should be cheap.

Sport Desmo 350, 500

The Desmo version of the vertical twin is more what Ducati enthusiasts would have expected the factory to provide in the first place, if it had to build one of these machines. Strangely the Sport Desmo was the creation, at least from a styling point of view, of Italjet boss Leo Tartarini. Also the majority of the machines were built at the Italjet plant, also in Bologna, rather than the Ducati factory. This stange set of circumstances came from a realization that with

the GTL Ducati had made a major mistake. So they called in Tartarini to solve the problem (he also styled the Darmah!). Compared with the very middle-of-the-road everyman's motorcycle of the GTL concept, the Sport Desmo was seen to be far more what a Ducati should be, at least to the press.

Motorcycle Mechanics tester John Robinson called the 500 version: "Ducati's Little Dictator," and went on the say: "The undeniable good looks of Ducati's 500 Sport has all the finely-styled contours you'd expect of a thoroughbred."

The Dictator tag stemmed from its Jekyll and Hyde-type character, which Robinson summed up in the following way: "When things go well, the Desmo twin howls along perfectly with a crisp response which makes you want to ride along with one hand protectively clutching your driving licence. When it's good, it's very very good . . . But push the 500 into doing something it doesn't want to do and the highly strung engine will throw an instant tantrum!"

Perhaps the biggest single problem of the Sport Desmo models, particularly the 350, was its extremely narrow power band. A six-speed

The production version of the 500 Desmo Sport vertical twin on display at 1976 Earls Court Show.

The very pretty, but underpowered, 350 "Desmo"
Sport — same size and weight as the 500.

Final Bologna vertical twins, the 350 GTV . . .

gearbox would have helped. Following closely on the heels of this was the *awful* finish of the exhaust system. Unlike the GTL models, the desmo twins had a matt black finish which even on bikes a mere week old was rusting in British weather.

As the *MCM* test concluded at its end: "You could go through the machine and produce a list of faults and imperfections, which would not look good at all. On one of the bland Japanese models they would attract far more criticism than I've aimed at the Ducati. This is solely because the Ducati isn't bland and isn't aimed at a rider whose sole contribution is to wind open the twist grip. It contrives to put character into both the motorcycle and into motorcycling, which, in my view, is worth a lot. Apart from saying that the 500 Sport is far from an everyday workhorse, I see little point in criticizing the machine. You can be fully aware of its problems and still think it's a great bike."

What to look for
Again, like the GTLs, very few Sport Desmos

were sold outside Italy, although some went to France; even fewer (around 50) went to Britain. But unlike the touring GTL, the Sport Desmos are much more closely related, at least in riding fun, to the ohc singles and V-twins. Therefore it will be harder to find one, at least one in anything like original condition and sound mechanically. Also, parts are a problem. You can't go into your friendly local Ducati dealer and expect to get much off the shelf, as except for a few items like brake pads and electrical bits, nothing is the same as on the other models. But it is still possible to get those vital parts if you know where to look. In Britian R & M Walker specialize in parts for these models, or you try could try an Italian dealer based near the factory.

Luckily, like the GTL, there wasn't the mass of changes found in some Ducati models through their production life span. Compared to the GTLs, the sportsters had cast alloy wheels, triple disc brakes, modified frame, clip-ons and rearsets and, of course, a totally different style and Desmo valve gear.

. . . and 500 GTV, appeared in 1978. Both featured uprated gearboxes, cast alloy wheels and minor cosmetic changes.

Star rating: Three stars
These are by far the most notable models of their type. And therefore justify a much higher rating.

Both the 350, with its striking yellow/black, and 500 in red/white show that Tartarini got his styling act together and transformed a potentially boring, unexciting bike into an out-and-out sportster.

I can't see either of the Sport Desmos being as collectable as a desmo single or 900 SS, but even so it's fun to ride, different and acts like the best Ducatis – what is good is brilliant, whats is bad is *really* bad.

That is why I award three stars.

GTV 350, 500
These were the final variation of the Ducati vertical-twin theme – virtually a marriage of the best bits from the GTL and Sport Desmos.

The result was a good, solid, reliable bike which ultimately lost out because it appeared at a time when the Pantah was being launched.

The main specification included Japanese switchgear, Bosch headlight, stainless steel mudguards, black outer engine covers, touring bars, revised foot controls, Darmah dual-seat (longer than the Sport Desmo), chrome exhaust system, new side panels, triple discs, cast alloy wheels, Sport Desmo twin down-tube frame and stainless steel chain-guard.

Even though, from specification and quality of finish, the GTVs were probably the *best* of the vertical twin Ducatis, they were even less successful than their predecessors. But this was simply that the Pantah had arrived and with it the final acceptance by the Ducati management that their great dream of increased sales through new customers for a different type of bike had finally failed.

What to look for
No hard and fast rules here, but because it's essentially a touring bike, the GTV falls into the same category as the GTL. But having said that the later bike is a much better one. Like all the verticals they are thin on the ground outside Italy and currently no one is trying very hard to dig them out. And compared to the more classic Ducati types the vertical twin will probably not have been so well looked after. Invariably when Ducatis are used as everyday transport they tend to deteriorate quickly.

Star rating: Two stars
Although, as stated, these are the best of the bunch, they only rate two stars as they are never going to be collector's items. The last batch was made in 1983; no one at the factory seemed keen on constructing them, it was simply that a quantity of engine units were on the shelf gathering dust!

Conclusion
A costly and embarrassing error by the Ducati management – and one which probably hasn't been forgotten. Ducati's buyers want something which they can accept as a Ducati, not something that a marketing man *assumes* they will want . . .

Chapter 11

Darmah

★ ★ ★	**Darmah SD 1977-83**
★ ★ ★ ★	**Darmah SS 1979-80**

History

Without a doubt the Darmah was the most important update on the Ducati big bike street scene (if one discounts the Pantah) since the introduction of the first 750s back in 1971. The Bologna company saw the Darmah project as the machine with which it could widen its market appeal, without falling into the trap suffered by the vertical twin described in the previous chapter.

Although retaining the classic bevel-driven 90-degree V-twin engine layout, the newcomer was none-the-less a substantial redesign, both from a mechanical and styling viewpoint. With this in mind the factory's engineers strove to not only achieve the above-mentioned priorities but at the same time to provide a higher level of sophistication and overall finish. All this without sacrificing Ducati's major asset, the *rideability factor.*

The Bologna Show in December 1976 was the launchpad for the public unveiling of the production prototype. This received an enthusiastic reception from both press and public alike, with production getting underway in the spring of 1977. Export markets had to wait longer.

Instantly noticeable was the dramatic styling, with an attractive red and white finish and gold Campagnolo cast alloy wheels. This was the work of Italjet boss Leopoldo Tartarini, and closely followed the successful formula the same man had adopted to transform the Ducati vertical twins into exciting machines a few months earlier. Just as he had achieved with the smaller machine, Tartarini's creative design talents endowed the new V-twin with an extremely sleek and slim look for what was after all a large-capacity motorcycle.

Also evident were a host of civilizing touches like the all-new instrumentation and switchgear (courtesy of the Japanese company Nippondenso), all new electronic ignition (Bosch), powerful 170 mm quartz halogen headlamp (Bosch again!), a new gear selector mechanism for.the five-speed gearbox, a new electric starter, new horn, larger-capacity 32-amp hour battery, stronger alternator, double-skinned exhaust pipes – and those previously mentioned Campagnolo cast alloy wheels.

At first glance the frame assembly could be mistaken for the earlier 860 GT/GTS type, but in reality it had been modified to offer a lower (29-in.) seat height – although it retained the former model's eccentric rear chain adjustment.

In the engine department the major change was that the gear selector box, formerly mounted outboard of the gearbox sprocket on the offside of the engine, had been dispensed with, and a completely new selector mechanism installed *inside* the engine on the opposite side. This meant that the cross-over shaft used previously to achieve a left-hand gearchange was therefore redundant. In theory it should have been a great improvement. But in practice, although marginally improving the gearchange, the set-up made locating neutral whilst stationary more difficult, and it did nothing to improve the heavy clutch action.

The Darmah was the first touring V-twin Ducati to feature desmodromic valve operation, whilst the new Bosch electronic ignition significantly improved the low-speed running characteristics. "Tourer" must be seen only when compared to other Ducatis, as the Darmah hardly rated the word in the conventional context; even though I'm sure the factory's design staff intended it as an everyday machine, they just couldn't alter its soul enough. The American journal *Cycle,* in their April 1980 test of the Darmah SD, put things into perspective perfectly, saying: "The Darmah is a civilized desmo, without the frame, fairing and other racetrack gilding of the Super Sport Desmo. But don't let that fool you. The V-twin engine – and the first winding road – will tell you the Darmah is the genuine Bologna article."

Model year 1977

When the Darmah was launched it created a great deal of attention on two counts – style and concept. The media were quick to appreciate that this was not merely a rehash but a major change in direction for the company, who at that time couldn't afford any more marketing failures after the succession of disasters over the previous couple of years (square-sided 860 GT, the chain-driven vertical twins and the 125 two-stroke enduro single).

But for once in their most recent history Ducati had judged the market perfectly. The result was a large amount of media attention, for all the right reasons, and strong initial sales of the new model.

Under the considerable improvements, though, civilization process if you will, there still remained at heart a torquey V-twin engine, sweet handling (although not *quite* up to the 750, 900 SS standard), and sure-footed braking, which had been the Ducati V-twin forté.

Compared to the latest crop of Japanese megabikes then arriving, 53 bhp may not have

The SD900 Darmah, named after a fabled Tiger in an Italian children's book, transformed Ducati's sales fortunes after it appeared in 1977.

84

appeared much, but unlike the majority of late 1970s Japanese machinery the Darmah was able to use what power it had to full advantage all the way through the power *and* torque scale.

By comparison the Japanese had yet to master the art of chassis design, with the result that machines such as the Yamaha XS1100, six-cylinder Honda CBX and Kawasaki Z1-R had engines which were far in excess of their frame capabilities. Only Suzuki, with the GS1000, could with any real safety be piloted to its full speed potential.

This was where the Darmah concept came in. In the past many potential owners had been put off buying the street racer 900 SS because it lacked items such as an electrical starter, air filters and relatively quiet silencers, not to mention inaccurate instruments and fiddly switchgear. With the Darmah, Ducati at last had a machine with which to attract these customers, whilst still remaining of interest to the dyed-in-the-wool Ducati man – who demanded a bike for the *sporting* rider.

In many ways, with its more laid-back style

– well at least it didn't have clip-ons and rearsets – performance figures and bhp curves didn't share the same importance as they would have done on an out-and-out sportster. What the press and new owners liked was its instant power delivery regardless of engine speed. The May 1978 issue of *Motor Cycle Mechanics* carried a Darmah test in which their tester said: "The outright power is not over-impressive, but the bars will pull from your grip when the throttle is snapped open, regardless of gear or the engines revs."

As for performance *MCM* got 113 mph, *Cycle* 116.3 mph.

Although most testers lauded the handling, several noted the use of a hydraulic steering damper (the first ever Ducati so fitted) and strange low-speed steering. But the majority were more than prepared to accept this for the much improved riding position offered by the almost flat handlebars, firm but low seat and excellent riding stance, compared with many earlier motorcycles from the Italian company.

What did let the Darmah SD down badly was the poor chrome plating on items such as

1980 SD900 changes included a new dual-seat, Silentium silencers, 315 mm gas shocks, an appropiate increase in length for centre-stand and Speedline cast alloy wheels.

The "Mark 2" Darmah SD dual-seat, with lockable plastic rear loop.

the headlamp brackets (on these it was truly awful!), kickstart lever, exhaust pipe/silencer clamps and indicator stems. The paintwork, although generally much improved, was prone to chipping on the glass-fibre side panels and seat base. Although better the finish still wasn't good enough!

Model year 1979

The first changes appeared that year. An SD Sport was introduced in a black and gold finish, with larger 40 mm carburettors and (usually) less restrictive Conti silencers – both items from the 900 SS parts bin. Unfortunately, in typical Ducati fashion, the cylinder head inlet ports were not opened out to match the larger carburettors . . . naughty!

Hard on the heels of the SD Sport came the lovely Darmah SS (Super Sport). This was a machine which bridged the gap between the standard Darmah SD/SD Sport and the pure street racer 900 SS.

The Darmah SS, distinctive with its ice blue/dark blue livery, was essentially the latest version of the 900 SS (now utilizing the Dar-

The much loved and popular Darmah SS finished in an attractive ice blue metallic: it was only built during 1979-80. Most were fitted with Conti silencers, rather than the Lafranconis shown.

86

mah gear selector mechanism and Bosch electronic ignition, but without the electric starter), 40 mm carburettors and Contis (although a few early Darmah SSs had 32 mm carbs/Lafranconi seamed silencers) mounted in a Darmah frame suitably modified with rear set foot controls.

Other differences besides the carburettors (which on the 40 mm instrument dispensed with the normal Darmah flip-up handlebar-mounted choke lever and restrictive silencers) and of course the different colour scheme included clip-ons, a 900 SS-type fairing and more rounded stainless steel mudguards.

All Darmah SD models from 1979 onwards dispensed with the back-up kickstarter. Although this did away with a reserve facility, it wasn't too unpopular – simply because the curved lever had been roundly disliked. A typical press comment had been: "A source of some nasty shin bites" (*Cycle World*).

Model year 1980
A number of changes were introduced, but only for the SD and SD Sport, not the SS. The most noticeable was the seating arrangement. This had been totally redesigned, both for additional comfort and storage space. Gone was the Tartarini-inspired swooping glass-fibre base with detachable seat section. In its place was a new type incorporating a plastic lift tail loop.

The seamed Lafranconis (and Contis on the SD Sport) had given way to extra quiet seamless Silentiums for, said the factory spokesman, "aesthetic reasons." There were longer 315 mm (original 300 mm) rear shock absorbers, of the gas-filled type. To compensate for this the centre-stand now had longer legs. But otherwise the Darmah still retained its unique appearance and was still in demand around the world.

Model year 1982
As the new decade dawned, it was accompanied by a drastic reduction in demand for new motorcycles. Ducati experienced declining sales during 1981, particularly with the Darmah SD. Both the Sport and SS version had been deleted from the range at the end of 1980. In an attempt to stimulate flagging demand the bi-annual Milan Show staged in

November 1981 saw the introduction of a new colour scheme and a range of factory accessories for the Darmah. The colour chosen was in stark contrast to the flamboyant red and white of the original. Why, or who, chose the unattractive deep burgundy is not known, but, whoever it was, he couldn't have conceived a less effective one!

The optional extras were hardly better received, the general feeling being that they were too little too late, and in any case were already available from other, cheaper sources. For the record, items made available were, colour-matched cockpit fairing, rear carrier and panniers.

Model year 1983
By now sales were down to a trickle. The last of the line, the 1983 SD, sported yet another colour scheme, gunmetal grey (the same as that year's 900 S2), but otherwise nothing else had been changed. Predictably sales were poor, with the result that by the middle of the year the model which had been such a success for the company a few short years before was killed off, after a reign of some six-years.

This coincided with the historic Ducati/Cagiva press conference at the beginning of June 1983, described elsewhere, which heralded in a new era for both companies. What was to begin as a courtship ended less than two years later in a full marriage.

What to look for
Darmahs tend to be found in one of two con-

The final Darmah SDs were offered with the choice of optional fairing, panniers and rear carrier during 1982-83.

ditions. The first is where the machine has been owned throughout its life by a traditional Ducati enthusiast. This person will have lavished it with love and attention, so preserving both its originality and mechanical condition. The other is where the previous owners would really have been more suited to either a Japanese bike or even a car. These people have used the bike as their sole means of daily transport, usually through all weathers. Now, up to ten years later, the machine is in need of a total cosmetic and mechanical restoration. In my experience it is far more economical to opt for the first type, even though it will mean a considerably higher outlay initially.

Like other Ducatis even an immaculate example needs careful vetting – the Darmah is no exception.

Among particular points to look out for is the starter sprag clutch. This is a one-way operating bearing, which is prone to fall apart and, remember, except for the very early example, the Darmah didn't have a back-up kickstarter.

Wheels can be another problem. The original excellent Campagnolos were soon replaced by ones from the Speedline company, which unfortunately, were subject to a spate of failures. 1979 was the main problem period, with many owners having wheels replaced under warranty. As these are liable to break up, anyone who still has Speedline cast alloy wheels on his Ducati (regardless of whether it is a Darmah) is advised to check now!

Finally Ducati made a third, and successful change, to FPS wheels.

Every large-bore Ducati V-twin with cast alloy wheels can suffer cush drive problems. The bolts that fix the cush unit to the rear wheel can come loose. If this is left unattended the only cure is a new wheel, but if noticed quickly enough the cure is to drill out the wheel to the next bolt size and use countersunk Allen screws.

Tyre wear, certainly by modern Superbike standards, is acceptable, with 6,000 miles possible on the rear and almost double that from the front cover.

The Darmah models are particularly sensitive about tyres. Metzelers and Dunlops do not seem to suit the model; much better are Avon Super Venoms, Michelin A38/M48 or Pirelli Phantoms. But ultimately it may be down to the individual rider's choice.

Like the other bevel-driven 860 V-twins, the gearbox can be a problem, and it should be noted that Ducati, in an attempt to improve matters, introduced a new design for the 1982 model year. But like the big-end assembly the key to longer life is regular oil changes – every 1,500 miles is recommended together with the correct oil, either a good-quality 20/50 (10/40 winter) multigrade or straight 40 (30 summer).

Another source of problems can be the transparent fuse box situated under the fuel tank, for, without protection, this can become filled with water, causing problems.

Star rating: SD and SD Sport three stars, SS four stars
The original Darmah concept, was, unlike many others made by the same management team during the mid/late 1970s, an inspired move. But even though the design was a sales success I cannot see the Darmah becoming a collector's bike, with the possible exception of the SS variant. Not only was this closer to the 750/900 SS models, but it was also made in far smaller numbers and over a much shorter period than the standard models. It's also a very attractive *sporting* motorcycle in its own right.

Chapter 12

Mike Hailwood Replica

★ ★ ★ ★	**MHR 1979**
★ ★ ★	**MHR 1980-86**

History

The Mike Hailwood Replica (or MHR) stemmed directly from the legendary British rider's triumphant return to the Isle of Man TT in 1978, when he scored a dramatic and famous victory aboard a specially prepared road racing version of the 900 SS. Essentially Hailwood's race win was a major stroke of luck for Ducati, as it generated a fantastic amount of publicity all around the world. And for once the beleaguered Ducati management made the right decision and capitalized with a model named after the feat.

Launched in 1979, essentially this was a customized and restyled 900 SS, finished in the colourful red, green and white livery of Hailwood's winning machine.

The first batch of Mike Hailwood Replicas of which some 500, were produced and 200 imported into Britain, all came with a certificate of authenticity. Soon the factory realized that they had struck gold and the model was put into general production to meet the demand, a demand which lasted longer than anyone at the time could have reasonably expected, until the mid-1980s. In fact it became the Bologna marque's best seller in the early 1980s, and sold well not only in Britain but also in West Germany and Japan.

Cashing in on a name

As *Motor Cycle* said in the test it carried out shortly after the model's début in 1979: "The Japanese can build bigger, faster, harder-accelerating rocket ships than this Ducati . . . but none can compete with a Hailwood Replica when it comes down to doing things in style." Tester Graham Sanderson (now in charge of Press and Public Relations at Honda's Chiswick, London, Headquarters) openly admitted that all he wanted to write down about the MHR were adjectives of admiration, words like "magnificent," "mean," "beautifully functional," "professional," and "artistic". But even Sanderson realized that a more objective train of critical thought must first be applied to the Italian sportster.

Apart from several obvious additions (and deletions) the MHR was in reality a 900 SS, with its price tag raised by just under 10 per cent. The model's striking feature was the bright red, green and white bodywork, but while sharing the same colour scheme as Hailwood's bike, it was not a true replica in appearance, let alone mechanically. One of the cleverest ideas on the Replica was the seat which could be converted from a single, large-humped racer to a dual bum pad. A section of the rear hump had three screws holding it (and the seat) in place. Remove these and the rear of the seat was revealed. Replace the three screws and you're away. The only manufacturer to come up with a better idea (at the time the MHR made its début) was MV Agusta, who had a neat sliding rear hump on a couple of models. Right at the very tail of the seat was the tool kit and room for a thin oversuit.

An unfortunate feature of the original fairing was its one-piece construction, which wrapped right around underneath the bike and did not have quick-release catches. This made routine maintenance tasks such as checking the oil level impossible without removing the fairing. This under-section area also acted as a water trap, but this problem was easily solved by simply drilling a few holes in its base. But it was effective in shape, penetrating the wind with no trace of instability, and was securely mounted at the front, at the sides and at the top, at the last point by a forged alloy stay mounted to the steering head nut.

The original version also came with a 24-litre glass-fibre petrol tank. But for Britain a smaller 18-litre metal tank was provided, with a glass-fibre cover. The lack of side panels gave instant access to the Yuasa battery on the right, and rear carburettor on the left, but not a lot of security; and as *Bike's* Dave Calderwood remarked: "The front carburettor is tucked away inside the fairing so deeply that it re-

quires the arm and wrist of a rose-jointed monkey to perform the necessary action of tickling the carburettor for cold starts."

Like the 900 SS, the MHR had no choke or air filters to the 40 mm Dell'Ortos, just a wire mesh grill to fend off inhaled debris, such as leaves, stones or other nasties.

The basic mechanics, such as the engine, chassis and front suspension, were identical to the SS, but the rear shocks were 20 mm longer. This was to accommodate the extra 17 kg weight of the fairing, larger tank, brackets, etc.

Proof of the fairing's good aerodynamics, even with the extra weight, was shown in the ability of the Replica to run up to the red line in fifth gear in the maximum speed tests carried out by the various magazines and I have confirmed this by personal experience.

The MHR came with SS gearing, having a 15/36 final drive ratio. *Bike* recorded a maximum speed of 132.1 mph, *Motor Cycle* 133.49 mph. During their speed testing at MIRA (Motor Industry Research Association) circuit, *Bike* had a Suzuki GSX1100 and Replica out together. In sheer performance terms the

Following Mike Hailwood's tremendous victory in the 1978 TT, Ducati decided to cash in the following year by launching the Mike Hailwood Replica. The first batch came with a certificate and one-piece fairing.

90

Suzuki proved superior, recording 137 mph and 11.3 seconds (against 132 mph and 12.5 seconds). What these figures concealed, however, was that on the Ducati the rider tucked in behind the fairing in, for that bike, the normal riding position. On the Suzuki at that speed, it was necessary to lie flat on the tank, feet on the pillion footrests and clutch hand off the bar and on to the fork stanchion, to get as much body as possible out of the wind to avoid being blown off the bike!

Today, with just about every Japanese big-bore sportster (read racer replica) sporting a comprehensive piece of streamlining, one is hard pressed to remember that besides Ducati and their "Mike-the-Bike" lookalike, only BMW (with the R100RS) and Moto Guzzi (SP Spada) offered fully faired bikes in 1979.

A worthwhile difference between the SS and the MHR was the latter's improved Nippondenso instrumentation and switchgear. But Ducati, in typically bizarre fashion, decided to have the red generator warning light glowing when it was working correctly, and it was only extinguished when there was

either a malfunction or the ignition was switched off! Another small detail was the brake calipers, which were anodized gold instead of black, but otherwise were identical.

Because of the full fairing, engine noise from all those whirring bevel gears tended to be reflected back at the rider. As soon as you sat astride the Replica, it was easy to imagine its racer role, since it had that same cobbled-together feel, not that it was a "bitza," but every component gave the impression that it was only there to fulfil some essential function. Like the SS, the clip-ons automatically placed the rider in a semi-racing crouch, completed when you finally got tucked in behind the one-piece fairing and screen. The long, slim (at least at the rear) tank moulding forced you back a fair way so, at least for shorter riders, it was quite a stretch to the bars.

As related, the very success of the Mike Hailwood Replica ensured its elevation, like the 900 SS, from a small-batch operation to the nearest thing to mass production in Ducati's book.

The 1980 version was essentially the same

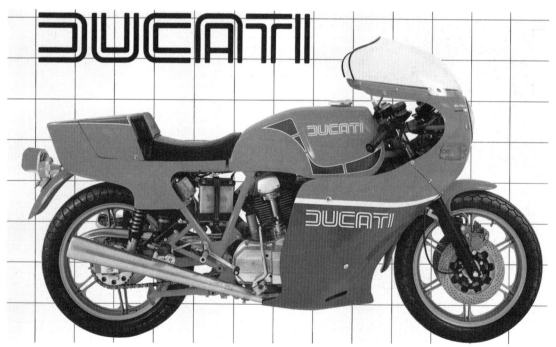

1980 saw the MHR enter "mass production" to meet the high demand. The most noticable change from the original was three-piece fairing.

The engine of the 1981 model Hailwood Replica. All versions had a red frame.

as the original, except for the substitution of a three-piece fairing. With each side removable separately, the previously poor access for servicing had been answered.

1981 saw more changes. There were quieter Silentium silencers, side panels, a larger 24-litre metal tank for all markets and a few other very minor differences. Ducati claimed that performance remained unchanged, but this is open to question with the more restrictive silencers.

The 1982 model year was distinguished by the MHR being equipped with side panels for the first time. This provided some protection for the battery and certain other electrical components.

Then in 1983 the machine received a major revamp, at least cosmetically. There were new side panels, fairing, front mudguard (now black to match rear mudguard), larger rear light, a different design and make of cast alloy wheels, oblong direction indicators, which were no longer integrally mounted at the front in the fairing, new instrument console and a black chainguard (formerly in polished stainless steel). And the engine now sported revised outer casings.

A hydraulic clutch appeared in 1984. The following year, in line with the S2, the engine capacity was enlarged to 973 cc and the machine renamed Mille Replica Desmo (although the colourful Mike Hailwood decals still appeared on the fairing). Cosmetically the 1985 bike retained the appearance of the 1984 version. Unlike the S2 Mille, the Mille Replica continued to be produced *after* the Cagiva

The 1983 MHR came with side panels plus *black* mudguards.

takeover in May 1985, and it was displayed on the company's stand at the Milan Show in November that year.

Early in 1986, the new owners finally axed the by now ageing bevel-driven Vee. And so, as the last Mille Replica rolled off the Bologna production line, the end of an era had been reached on an engine type which had made its début back in 1971 as the 750 GT.

What to look for

First determine if the model you have your eyes on is the *real* thing. This is more important than you may think – there are several replica Replicas around. I've even seen converted Darmahs offered as Hailwood Replicas!

So do the basics, check it's got the pukka SS-type frame. Another pointer is the Darmah-type Nippondenso instrumentation (no SS models, except the Darmah SS, had these), and that the frame is red. Finally check the registration document for both description and frame/engine number.

As the Replica was built up until very recently and sold in quite large numbers, it is still possible to find pristine examples.

Star rating: 1979 MHR four stars; 1980-86, three stars

These star ratings are solid, so maybe they should have a "plus" mark beside them. I'm sure as time goes by genuine Mike Hailwood Replicas are destined to climb in value. Cur-

The 1984 model, just before the final 1000 Mille version appeared. It had many changes including louvered side panels, new rear light, indicators and fairing, outer engine castings, and hydraulic clutch.

rently there are simply too many around to score higher marks than I've awarded.

As a fellow journalist once said: "While Ducati's Hailwood Replica might not conform to the Oxford Dictionary definition of an exact copy by the same artist, it certainly helped me emulate the maestro's style."

Footnote

A final note on the "genuine" 1978 TT-winning Hailwood racer(s). I was recently asked to give a value on this bike. But quite simply it was impossible, for there were at least *four* bikes in the Isle of Man. Of course their respective owners all claim to have the actual race bike. The truth is *nobody* really knows, a decade later, which was used in the race.

Chapter 13

Pantah

★ ★ ★	**500 SL 1979-83**
★ ★ ★	**600 SL 1981-83**
★ ★ ★	**650 SL 1983**
★ ★	**600 TL 1982-83**
★	**350 XL 1982-83**
★ ★ ★	**350 SL 1982-83**

History

Internal management politics played a major part in the conception of the Pantah series. Ducati's legendary design genius, Ing. Taglioni, was pushed very much into the backwaters of the management structure within the Bologna factory for a period in the mid-1970s. How wrong this policy turned out to be is amply illustrated by just how much money was lost on the development of "new concept" bikes which didn't sell, and by 1977 the old man was back in favour.

In retrospect, many would argue that had Taglioni not been stifled the Pantah would have appeared significantly earlier and not at the end of 1978 as events transpired.

Back in 1975 Taglioni had planned a series of modular motorcycles, not only to fill a void left by the disappearance of the long-running bevel-driven ohc singles, but also to provide a series of middleweight V-twins of various engine capacities.

However, because of several factors, these new machines needed to be more economical to produce and also be able to meet the ever-increasing governmental legislation on environmental issues, such as noise and pollution. Therefore the design had to be suitable not only for the late 1970s but the next decade as well.

But his new range of singles and V-twins never got any further than the drawing board, that was until early in 1977, by which time it

had become obvious, even to those sections of the management who had backed the 1975 "new concept" plan, that *none* of their models was going to be a sales success (that is the single-cylinder two-stroke enduro, the vertical twins and the Giugiaro-styled 860 GT).

So Taglioni was authorized to proceed with all possible speed with his modular singles and V-twins. And the first fruits of his work were shown to the press and public at the Milan Show in November 1977, in the shape of two 350 singles and a 500 V-twin.

Ultimately the modular plan visualized a range of motorcycles from 250 to 750 cc, all using the same concept, a four-stroke engine with desmodromic valve operation, with toothed belt drive to the overhead camshafts, plain bearing big-ends and a high-pressure lubrication system incorporating a car-type full-flow filtering system.

Unfortunately, soon after the Milan début the Bologna management team were forced by their government bosses in Rome to reappraise the development programme, with the result that there were to be *no* singles and only authorizaton for the 500 V-twin. A proviso was made that if it was successful, other V-twins would be considered later. And so the first of the Pantahs, the 500 SL, was born.

500 SL

Although it shared the now familiar 90-degree "L-shape" layout, the Pantah V-twin was quite different in several important technical respects to the established bevel-driven Vees. Compared to these it was also smoother, quieter and more docile – the word best used to describe this change best is *civilized.*

The engine started at the touch of a button, every time and ticked over reliably at 1,000 revs; it was quieter than a BMW flat-twin, and it did not vibrate perceptibly at any engine speed.

Roadholding and handling were of the usual standard expected from the marque, even though the trellis frame, from which the engine hung, was radically different in design, with a considerably shorter wheelbase than that fitted to the other models in the Ducati range. The swinging arm assisted this move towards a shorter wheelbase by pivoting through the gearbox casing. In addition the gearbox sprocket was very close to the swinging arm pivot, cutting down on chain tension variations.

The 74×58 mm bore and stroke measure-

ments were virtually identical to the earlier bevel-driven 250 single (that was actually 74×57.8 mm). But unlike this machine, when it had made its bow back in 1961, by the late 1970s these short-stroke measurements were typical of many other manufacturers' sport engines.

The cooling fins were cast longitudinally on the horizontal cylinder, and circumferentially on the vertical, as on the larger twins, but now had numerous rubber inserts in the quest for quieter running.

The big-ends were side-by-side split white metal shells, while for the first time on a Ducati engine the helical gear primary drive was on the off-side. The car-type oil filter was located underneath the crankcases for easy access, and an instant check could be made of the oil level with an easy-to-read sight glass.

But it was the camshaft drive arrangement which was the most unusual, and as this was at the heart of the new design deserves a more detailed description. From the near-side (left)

The first batch of production Pantah 500 SLs appeared in 1979 and unlike later models finish was in red, with white striping.

The 1980 model 500 SL in ice blue with red/blue striping. This photograph shows the plastic seat hump removed for pillion use.

The 500 SL engine: note the oil level sump glass and low slung starter motor.

of the crankshaft a pair of helical-cut spur gears drove a half-time idler shaft which crossed to the off-side of the power unit along the crutch of the vee. On the end of this idler shaft was a toothed belt pulley which drove two separate belts, to their respective camshafts. The rear of each belt ran over a small fixed plain pulley on its working run, and over a

slightly bigger pulley mounted on an adjustable bolted-up plate on the return run. These pulleys, in typical Taglioni fashion, consisted simply of sealed ball races. In other words, the outer surfaces of the ball journals themselves served as pulleys. Road dirt and water were kept off the belts by cast alloy covers – which, of course, didn't have to be oil

The much improved 600 SL appeared in 1981 in silver with contrasting red stripes. It benefitted from stonger gearbox and hydraulic clutch.

96

tight.

Ignition like the Darmah and later 900s was by Bosch, with assistance from Nippondenso, Ducati Electronica and Yuasa (if you count the battery). Generally speaking, except for the infamous sprag clutch bearing (see Chapter 11), the mixture worked well. The gearbox used several components from the vertical twins and none from the bevel-driven vees. The rest of the engine unit was new.

Many usual Ducati components were used, including Dell'Orto pumper carburettors (36 mm), triple Brembo discs (260 mm), Marzocchi front forks (35 mm) and rear suspension units, Bosch headlamp (smaller 150 mm version of Darmah assembly), 18-in. cast alloy wheels and double-skinned exhaust pipes, with detachable balance pipe.

Electronically timed test results showed the 500 SL to have a genuine maximum speed just short of 120 mph and able to cover the standing quarter-mile in 13.51 seconds.

In two areas the 500 SL was *really* different to earlier Ducatis, style and silence.

Dennis Noyes when testing the new half-litre Ducati in the December 1980 issue of *Which Bike?* referred to the styling as: "A bit flash and extreme for some tastes." I think it is best described as "razor edge." Certainly the original fairing (changed in late 1980) was a distinct departure from that used on the pre-production prototype shown at Milan and Cologne (September 1978), which followed the rounded lines of the 900 SS. And for once the Silentium silencers *really* lived up to their name. It must be said that many Ducati buffs didn't (and still don't) appreciate the super quiet exhaust note. But whatever your views on the original Pantah, it did introduce a host of new acts into the Ducati repertoire.

What to look for

Early 500 SLs were not without their problems, notably the main bearings, gearboxes and the starter sprag clutch bearing. But except for the last named all these difficulties had been eliminated by the end of 1980, when the "Mark 2" version was introduced, identified by its 600 SL fairing and front mudguard (see the illustrations). My advice is always go for the later model if you have a choice, unless you are absolutely sure that the impovements

The hydraulic clutch of the 600 SL.

have been carried out to any earlier bike that you are considering. Otherwise, in my experience, the Pantah engine is most definitely more reliable than the bevel-driven vees. Not only this, but if things do go wrong, it is likely to be less expensive to put right. For example big-end shells and drive belts are but a fraction of the cost of components which do the same work in the older engine design: complete con-rod assemblies and matched pairs of bevel-drive gears respectively.

The 600 TL tourer was a sales flop. The unsold bikes were cleared at knock-down prices in certain export markets, including Britain.

97

Except for a manual clutch the TL engine was the same gutsy performer as the SL version.

Several 500 SLs (and other Pantahs for that matter) have been used as the basis for various TT F2 racer conversions – for both road and track. A word of warning here. Some of these are true works of art, whereas others (often home built) are less than perfect. Be *very* careful that you are buying the pukka thing and my advice is to opt for one built by a known specialist. There are also a host of different frames, usually monoshock; of the best known are Verlicchi (a virtual replica of the works racer) and Harris. Finally, my star ratings do not apply to these machines – be guided instead by the bike's history, quality of construction and existing condition.

Star rating: Three stars
This may at first glance seem a harsh marking

The tank and side panels on the 600 TL are best described as weird.

for a design which set new engineering ideas in motion. But the sales success of the various Pantah models has ensured that it is widely available and the motor in up-dated and enlarged form is still the basis of the very latest range of Superbikes from the famous Bologna marque. Therefore the 500 SL's three stars is the same as I awarded to the bike it replaced, the 500 Sport Desmo vertical twin, but for largely differing reasons. The earlier bike gained three stars for rarity, the 500 SL for quality. But most of all the model doesn't win a higher rating because it lacks the *character* of certain other Ducatis. In the final analysis it's maybe just *too* modern in concept, both in style and execution.

600 SL 1981-83
Much of what has been said above applies equally to this model, but besides its larger capacity, 583 cc (80 × 58 mm), and extra power, up from 45 to 60 bhp, the 600 SL engine offered other advantages. Torque figures were increased from 4.07 kg/m at 8,000 rpm to 5.17 kg/m at the lower engine speed of 7,500 rpm. And to cope with this additional power and torque the clutch was upgraded and hydraulically operated (for the first time on a Ducati). Although maximum speed was only about 4 mph greater, and the rest of the engine, including the carburettor size, was as before, the 600 was a superior machine thanks to its greater flexibility, and of course its impoved gearbox (also incorporated in the 500 version at the same time).

The silver colour scheme combined well with the restyled fairing and new front mudguard to give a greatly improved appearance.

What to look for
Nothing to add here from that already stated in the 500 SL section.

Star rating: Three stars
Compared to the smaller SL, the 600 has to be a better buy, but it's also likely to be considerably more expensive and harder to find, therefore it still gets the same star rating.

650 SL 1983
This was the last of the Pantahs before the

major update and enlargement to 750 for models like F1 and Paso. It had even more torque than the 600 version. Very few were actually produced. The finish was a very attractive red/yellow, the same colours adopted for works TT F2 racers of the world championship years. Bore and stroke were both revised (82×61.5 mm) to give 649 cc and 66 bhp, but otherwise it was unchanged from 600 SL.

What to look for

Nothing much to add, except to say that it was a pity that Ducati only used the colour scheme, and not the style, from their works racers . . .

Star rating: Three firm stars

More desirable, if only because of even more punch and rarity, but as it's so similar to the other SL models in appearance it is not worth an additional star.

600 TL

Launched together with the 350 XL, the 600 TL first went on sale in Italy during the spring of 1982. This was intended as the touring Pantah (also for police duties in modified form). Mechanically, except for a manual clutch, it is the same as the SL. But in styling it is vastly different from the sports model. In place of the clip-ons were a pair of slightly raised conventional handlebars, the sports fairing was replaced by a much smaller bikini fairing with a tinted screen which offered only minimal protection, there were revised footrests and controls, and a very comfortable-*looking* dual-seat. The bodywork extended down to cover the top half of the Desmo engine and there was a completely revised instrument console, with Veglia clocks (a few machines had Nippondenso). A range of matching accessories including Krauser panniers, and crashbars were also available as optional extras.

Lacking the charisma of the SL model, the TL proved a poor seller. As proof of this, several months after the machine had been taken out of production unsold examples were offered in Britain (and elsewhere), initially at £1,999, later rising to £2,199. These imports by Moto Vecchia during 1984-85 totalled some 100 machines. At these prices the TL represented excellent value, and with the exception of

The TL seat looks plush, but was just the reverse – after a few miles it felt like a plank of wood!

some relatively minor faults (such as the seating arrangement) proved popular. But this should be seen in the light that the British price was artificially low – a *real* price would have been at least a third higher.

As I discovered, when I tested a 600 TL for *Motorcycle Enthusiast* (March 1985), the plush-looking saddle spoilt an otherwise much underrated motorcycle. The motor of the test machine really impressed me, with its ability to fire up from cold, even after standing uncovered outside for four days of continual rain in late November. Every time it fired sweetly without the need for any choke. After a few blips of the throttle one could select first and ride off cleanly. To achieve this the only prerequisite was to open and shut the throttle twice before pressing the starter button, so as to allow the pumper Dell'Ortos to squirt

The final version of the SL, the 650, at the Cologne Show, September 1986.

enough fuel into the cylinders.

Once on the road the motor's response was brisk and, although torquey, had a definite sporting edge. Its performance when revved hard to around 7,000 rpm in the gears was excellent. And I could fully appreciate just why Tony Rutter had been Formula 2 World Champion for the previous four years using a racing version of this power plant. It was powerful, smooth, forgiving and reliable. Maximum speed in touring trim was the high side of 110 mph. The riding stance was also perfect for my 5 feet 10 inches, with only that seat spoiling matters.

What to look for

Very few 600 TLs were produced, and even less ever went outside Italy. Those from the batch sold in Britain were mainly finished in a metallic gunmetal grey with orange stripes (the same colours as the 1983 900 S2), and the other colour option was white with red striping. Like the SL models, several (at least of those in Britain) were converted into TT F2 replicas.

Star rating: Two stars

Underneath the somewhat wierd "banana" styling lurked a basically excellent motorcycle. However, just as it wasn't popular when new, its lacklustre appearance does not endear it to collectors or enthusiasts now. But I still feel it deserves two stars, if only for its excellent engine and sheer rideability.

350 XL

A model produced exclusively to take advantage of Italy's tax laws, which saw a big jump in rates for bikes over 350 cc. This red and black machine was intended as a competitor to Guzzi's V35 and Morini's 3½, but never really made much impression in the sales war. The 348 cc (66 × 51 mm) engine produced a *claim-*

ed 40 bhp, but most observers thought this much nearer 30. In addition Taglioni himself openly admitted that its engine characteristics were too peaky. This is confirmed by the much lower torque figures, which were also higher up the scale, 3.42 kg/m at 8,500 rpm (maximum 9,600). Another feature of the design was the smaller 30 mm carburettors. Styling was similar to the 600 TL, but with the SL tank, seat and panels (why didn't the larger machine share this much superior styling package?)

What to look for

Exceptionally reliable engine, though lower stresses are about all this under-powered model has to commend it. In any case almost extinct outside its homeland.

Star rating: One star

Ducati's answer to BMW's R45!

350 SL

Basically 350 SL, but with full SL styling. Striking red and green paintwork. Small engine again lets it down. A few examples were specially prepared for Italian F3 racing. Sales were surprisingly successful for the short time it was available on the home market.

Star rating: Two stars

More attractive style and colours than the touring model, hence one more star.

Summary

Ing. Taglioni's last major design exercise, the Pantah series, restored something like success to a shell-shocked management prior to the Cagiva takeover. And without the Pantah engine I doubt if the Castiglioni brothers would have been interested in acquiring the Bologna concern anyway! So history will show that the Pantah saved Ducati from extinction.

Chapter 14

F1

★ ★ ★ ★	**F1 1985-87**
★ ★ ★ ★ ★	**Montjuich, Laguna Seca,**
	Santamonica 1985-87
★ ★ ★	**F3 1985-87**

History

To the true believer, the F1 (and to a lesser extent the smaller-engined F3), represents the last of the real Ducatis, in other words, the traditionally raw, sporting motorcycle, without an ounce of surplus fat anywhere to be seen.

And with its racer-like styling, the F1 evoked passion within Ducati enthusiasts the world over, whether they resided in Britain, North America, Australia, Japan or even Italy.

As the American journal *Cycle World* so aptly put it: "Ducati must have known that a line was about to be drawn in the history books, and the people there must have wanted to leave a last entry. Because the F1 is everything an Italian sportsbike is expected to be and so seldom is."

Behind this statement was a pedigree which could be traced directly back to Ducati's successful F2 and F1 racers. If the F1 project had a fault, it was that it should have appeared several years earlier. And by the time the factory got around to creating it, its racing brothers had already scored four World Championships (F2 category) and were all but consigned to the history books.

Of course the other reason why the F1/F3 models can truly lay claim to "last-of-the-line" title, is that they were the final designs to reach production before the Cagiva takeover in the spring of 1985.

The prototype of what was to emerge as the 750 F1 engine appeared in several long-distance endurance races in 1983, including the Le Mans 24 Hours.

F1 1985-87

Compromise is not a word which has ever figured very highly in Ducati's list of priorities; with the F1 it hardly appeared at all, making it one of the very best bikes ever to leave the Borgo Panigale factory gates.

Compared to the earlier bevel-driven vees, the belt-drive Pantah engine is definitely more reliable and the records of the F1 and F2 works racers only serve to back up this statement.

Ing. Taglioni's development team had already stretched the modular-concept Pantah V-twin first from 499 cc to 583 cc and then to 649 cc. But with the 750 (actually 748 cc) it grew even more. This was achieved by using the 650's stroke of 61.5 mm and adding 6 mm to the bore, giving 88 mm, these vastly over-square dimensions allowing the larger engine to rev higher than perhaps many had expected it might. Like the 600 and 650, the 750 featured a hydraulic clutch and several improvements which had been made over the years since the original Pantah had been introduced.

But in many ways, as with the racers, it was the chassis rather than the power unit which created the most interest. Like the works bikes, this followed the basic principles of using the engine as a stressed member thanks to its very strong gravity diecast crankcases.

The round-section swinging arm pivoted in the rear of the crankcases (as on the earlier road-going Pantahs, too) before coming up to meet the cantilever rear suspension.

In fact, even in appearance, the frame, rather than the engine, dominated the bike. Perhaps this was to be expected when one realizes that with 57 bhp (or up to 63 depending on which dyno you believe) the F1's straight-line performance was significantly down on the Japanese racer replica 750s, which were by now putting out some 90 bhp on average. In fact several of the Oriental 600s produced more power.

But a low frontal area, narrow width and effective steamlining made the very best use of what power there was. With a timed maximum speed of 127 mph (*Performance Bikes*), the F1 was identical to BMW's K75S, which needed 75 bhp to achieve the same result.

At this point, combined with effective penetration, the chassis takes on more importance. It steered and handled like a thoroughbred racer and this enabled it to score heavily over the more sedate three-cylinder BMW, so between points A and B the Ducati was considerably quicker, even though it had less power and an identical maximum speed! This agility brought the F1 back into the region of performance occupied by the latest generation of Japanese sportsters. It is worth noting the importance of suitable tyres, for the F1 seems to prefer low-profile Michelin Hi-Sports or Pirelli Phantoms and other covers don't seem to suit as well.

Fitting these tyres only emphasizes the F1's biggest failing – its centre-stand. Obviously on what is basically a pure racing chassis a centre-stand has to be an add-on "extra", and it showed up badly by touching down far too easily when I tested an F1 back in 1986. If you are going to ride the bike in anything like the manner it was intended, my advice is to dump the centre-stand and substitute a side-stand (as fitted to the Montjuich/Santamonica).

Fashion dictated a 16-in. front wheel, but Ducati were loath to forsake their traditional stability, so kicked out the steering angle (rake)

The last of the raw boned, street racing "Dukes", the 750 F1, was available from mid 1985 to early 1988.

102

The smaller 350 F3 – same style, less performance. A 400 cc version was built specially for the Japanese market.

to 28 degrees, with a long 155 mm trail. Consequently the steering was a touch on the heavy side, but it was still possible to change direction quickly. The F1 needed its steering damper, hidden in among the fairing brackets and frame tubes, when really heavy bumps could set the front tyre kicking. These are the only faults, though, for otherwise its handling and roadholding are beyond reproach, performing in the same impeccable fashion whether threading your way through city traffic or negotiating high-speed swervery at over 120 mph.

The Marzocchi single-shock rear suspension, which followed the early Yamaha pattern, might not have been the modern rising rate variety, but was extremely compliant and matched any of the more sophisticated Japanese types currently on offer. You can ride the F1 anywhere, anytime, and not have to unduly avoid potholes or similar road irregularities, unlike the earlier Ducatis, such as the 900 SS or Hailwood Replica!

This fine combination of more travel and softer spring rates was one of the biggest

bonuses on the whole bike: the old bogey of overhard Italian suspension deleted in a single stroke.

"Brickwall"-type stopping power was provided by a pair of 280 mm floating Brembo discs up front, which tended to rustle

The endurance racing version of the 750 F1 at the Milan show, November 1985.

disconcertingly on their dowels at low speeds, with simple dual piston calipers. The single rear 260 mm disc for the same source kept the rear end firmly under control.

Early F1s had Marzocchi front forks, later models Forcella Italia (formerly Cerriani), but with either the stanchion diameter was a hefty 40 mm. These later machines also went to a Suzuki GSX-R style cockpit, an aircraft filler cap, Kokusan (instead of Bosch) electronic ignition, a dry clutch and revised graphics.

A 22-litre sheet-steel tank provided for a good range between stops, helped by a fuel consumption which could, with a little respect, easily show the plus side of 50 mpg; for example, *Performance Bikes* averaged 47 mpg and *Motorcycle International* 49 mpg, and don't forget these figures included all the various speed testing.

The fairing, with its relatively high screen, left the rider and the V-twin in a bubble of still air. The riding stance, even with the clip-ons and rear-sets, benefitted from a well-laid-out position and the shape, rather than the

padding, of the single seat. A few journalists decried the lack of a dual-seat option (later rectified), but in my opinion the F1 is a strictly "solo only" mount. It said a lot for the layout of such an uncompromising sportster that the rider was tolerably comfortable, and the harder you went, the better it became. This is proof, if any is needed, of the part which the positioning of controls and improved suspension played.

If the F1 had a major failing, it was its low power output. But against this the belt-driven Desmo engine was crisp and free running *and* torquey. And it still retained all the virtues of the big V-twin; the power delivery was rough enough to let you know something was happening, but the engine was smooth enough not to shake the bike to pieces or need sloppy rubber mounts everywhere.

As the power curve proved, the F1 was in a mild state of tune, with peak torque well down the rev scale, between 4,500 and 5,000 rpm. There was a flat spread of torque through to 7,000, at which point the engine had a really solid throttle response. Beyond this speed the

Limited, hand built F1, the stylish and speedy Laguna Seca, circa 1987.

104

load trailed off progressively until the power just stopped, somewhere above 9,500 rpm.

It is tempting to conclude that a fiercer cam profile, or a small revision of cam timing, would have been preferable, as this would have offered a fairly profound effect at the top end of the performance range, but for normal road use this would have robbed the engine of its superb flat torque curve and, in particular, its mid-range punch.

But there was another reason why Ducati didn't take this course. This was because a more sporting version (or more correctly *versions* of the F1) was offered alongside it.

Called, depending on the dates they were offered, alternatively, Montjuich, Laguna Seca and Santamonica, these were hand-built *real* race replicas for racing, or fast road work. But as they were only made in very limited numbers and were at least 25 per cent more expensive than the standard F1, they are very rare indeed.

These were clearly based more closely on the works F1 racers, with 40 mm (some Montjuichs retained 36 mm instruments)

Dell'Ortos, 10:1 (standard 9.3:1) compression pistons, bigger valves and a less restrictive exhaust. They pushed out power from 7,500 through to over 10,000 rpm and put it through the stock transmission, although with straight cut (like the works bikes) instead of helical primary drive gears.

The gearbox was fully capable of withstanding the need to keep the engine spinning between 7,500 and 10,000, which in itself was quite an achievement when one considers the gearbox problems on tuned bevel-driven 900s. And there was little doubt that the chassis was able to cope with the extra power, as the standard F1 handled like a racer.

Quite often these special F1s came with pukka slick racing tyres, indicating at least what the factory thought they should be used for – winning races! But, of course, in practice more found their way on to the street than the race circuit.

But prospective buyers must realise that these were strictly hand-built small-production machines and therefore did not have a "standard" specification – with even

The final variant of the F1 theme, the high performance Santamonica.

different carburettor sizes and types of tyre specified.

For North American roads the F1, in any form, was effectively outlawed as there was no place in the mid-1980s Stateside for a bike with such a raucous exhaust note and no trace of air filtration, let alone emissions controls. So instead all the F1s sold on that side of the Atlantic came shorn of their lights and turn signals, and marked "for racing use only".

Even so, they, like the other F1s, were quickly snapped up. After all these were (provided they could afford them!) just the bike so many Ducati enthusiasts has craved for. As *Cycle World* said: "They may be bargains. This last Ducati is a throwback in spirit to the 750 SS of 1973, the F1's most famous predecessor. Like the 750 SS, the F1 is *the* Italian sportsbike of its era."

With ever tightening regulations from all sides, many feared the F1 could be the last opportunity to purchase a motorcycle with such a pure heart.

What to look for

By now you will have realized that I'm more than sold on the F1 concept, as are many other Ducati buffs. This means that F1s don't remain with a "For Sale" ticket for long. They also seem to survive in better cosmetic *and* mechanical condition than their forerunners. This is probably because they weren't cheap and that they are more reliable.

Star rating: F1 four stars, Montjuich, Laguna Seca and Santamonica five stars

If you find, or already own, an F1 my advice is to hang on to it. If you are doubly lucky to have been able to afford one of the "limited edition" models, then guard it with your life, for you have a real classic of the future. Any one of the Montjuich, Laguna Seca or Santamonica models is worth five full stars, for they are both beautiful *and* rare.

F3 1984-87

Originally intended for home market consumption, the F3, like other 350 Pantahs, suffers badly with a much inferior power to weight ratio, compared to its bigger brothers. The F3 shared the same 349 cc capacity, and 66 × 51 mm bore and stroke measurements of the earlier 350 XL and SL Pantahs. Not only that, but an identical state of tune: 40 bhp at 9,600 rpm, although subsequently the output went up to 42 at 9,700. Ducati *claimed* a maximum speed of 108 mph, but in any case the biggest problem was sluggish acceleration and a generally gutless engine. The top speed once again proved the worth of the narrow frontal area and effective streamlining provided by the fairing, which was identical to the larger model.

Besides a colourful red and white colour scheme (no green this time), there were smaller diameter (35 mm) Marzocchi front forks, Bosch ignition system on all versions, a mechanically operated clutch, narrower-section tyres and 260 mm discs all round.

A few F3s (with the engine capacity increased to 400 cc) found their way to Japan, which, strange as it may seem, was, by the mid-1980s, Ducati's best export market. But the smaller model never achieved any real success, living very much in the shadow of its illustrious bigger brother.

What to look for

Here, looks very much deceive, for underneath its flashy exterior the F3 is a real let-down, with its performance never remotely matching its racy lines. My advice is don't bother, for you will be sorely disappointed. The chassis and brakes cry out for more power, enough said?

Star rating: Three stars

Only earns an average rating – three stars – because of its lovely looks, but if it was a question of performance only it would be lucky to score one.

Chapter 15

The New Breed

★ ★ ★	**Paso**
★ ★	**Indiana**
★ ★ ★ ★	**851 Superbike**
★ ★ ★ ★	**750 Sport**

History

Following Cagiva's acquisition of Ducati Meccanica on 1 May, 1985, a whole new era was about to begin for the famous Bologna marque. For many, many years Ducati had struggled under a succession of government-appointed managers, but had found very little commercial success, a stark contrast indeed from its growth during the same period to the level of a "cult" for many enthusiasts around the world.

Not only was Cagiva's financial muscle to be applied to the ailing company, but at the same time a trio of men were to emerge from the shadow of that great Ducati designer Ing. Fabio Taglioni, who had officially "retired" at the end of 1982. These were Ing. Massimo Bordi, ex-racer and development engineer, Franco Farne, and co-founder of Bimota, Massimo Tamburini.

Bordi had joined Ducati in January 1978 following a period at University, a couple of years as a teacher and afterwards employment in the Quality Control Department of the Terni plant.

Farne had been a Ducati employee from as long ago as 1950, when he had joined direct from school at 16 years old. He had ridden against some of the world's finest riders until 1963, when a serious injury had ended his racing career, and from that time on had been one of Taglioni's right-hand men in the Research and Development Department.

Meanwhile the third member of the trio, Massimo Tamburini, co-founder of Bimota and its chief designer for over a decade, had been recruited by Cagiva in early 1985. However, unlike Bordi and Farne, Tamburini was not directly involved with Ducati, or for that matter to be seen at work at the Bologna factory. Instead he worked at his own styling studio.

The first major programme involving all three men was the Paso. Two of these bikes (a 750 and 350) were launched at the Milan Show in November 1985, together with the semi-chopper-styled Indiana custom bike.

A couple of years on and the long-awaited 851 Superbike made its bow at Milan, followed up in the spring of 1988 by an old name, the 750 Sport, in reality an undressed and lightly tuned Paso, in an F1 frame.

By the time I wrote this chapter (summer 1988), Ducati were well on the way to re-establishing themselves as leaders of the Italian large-capacity sports bike manufacturing table, after a long spell in the wilderness.

Paso 1986-

Although it was displayed to the public in prototype form in late 1985, it was not until 1986 that anybody could purchase one.

The enclosed bodywork Paso was extremely radical when it first appeared – remember this was over a year ahead of Honda's similarly styled CBR600 and 1000 models.

The name Paso was in recognition of famous Italian racing star Renzo Pasolini – known to his countless fans as simply "Paso". Particularly noted for his exploits on Benelli and Aermacchi machines, this great sportsman was tragically killed in the accident at Monza in May 1973 which also claimed the life of the flying Finn Jarno Saarinen.

So how come Ducati, for whom Pasolini never raced, came to name a bike after him? Simple, the new owners of Ducati, Cagiva, bought the old Aermacchi–Harley-Davidson Varese plant in September 1978 and decided to honour their hero on the first new bike after Cagiva took over Ducati in 1985.

Although its styling was the most obvious departure from previous models, the 748 cc (88×61.5 mm) Pantah engine available from 1989 as the "906", in fact 904 cc (92×68 mm), was also considerably up-dated, including an improved 14-plate dry clutch and Japanese Kokusan electronic ignition. By reversing the rear cylinder head of the belt-driven engine, a single-choke Weber 44 DCNF carburettor was used. Besides its excellent performance, this had the added advantage of a much improved

(read lighter!) action, thanks to its butterfly, rather than cylindrical, slide.

The combination of a giant airbox, super quiet Silentium silencers and the all-enveloping plastic bodywork ensured a level of silence unknown in any previous Ducati.

There is no doubt that the Paso was conceived as a motorcycle which could sell in any market, and maybe to almost any type of potential customer – something its traditional, noisier, less civilized brothers could never do.

However, although generally the world's press raved about it, the Paso was not as perfect as these journalists would have us believe. For example, that bodywork hid some of the worst welding ever seen outside Japan, and this same bodywork was far less effective at protecting its rider from the elements than it was as a reducer of engine noise levels.

The 16-in. front wheel exhibited the normal 16-in. front wheel trait – touch the brake in a corner and the bike stands upright. And although mid-range power was stronger than the F1, the Paso is still not in the same league as the latest Japanese 750 sportsters. Mike

Built for world-wide sales, the enclosed bodywork Paso 750, the first of the "new breed" which made its début in late 1985.

108

Clay, writing in the March 1987 issue of *Motorcycle Enthusiast*, put it this way: "Acceleration is brisk and satisfying, but anyone expecting to blitz the current crop of four-cylinder Japs is going to be sadly disillusioned."

Besides its styling, which you either loved or hated, the excellence of the suspension and the high level of finish were its biggest assets. *Motorcycle International* commented: "The smooth, bounce free ride afforded by the 42 mm (41.7 mm to be exact) Marzocchi forks (anti-dive in one leg only with adjustable air assistance) and Ohlins monoshock is so un-Italian that it all but defies belief."

Mike Clay, summing up at the end of his test report, said: "The Paso is a very fine, practical, sporting motorcycle, embodying a subtle blend of ultra-modern style with the pick of Ducati's traditional virtues. At £5,495 [the British launch price in 1987] it is £300 cheaper than the F1 and £2,500 less than the DB1 (Bimota). The only question mark hangs over just who will buy it. Will it appeal to the traditional Duke owner? Will it attract a new group of customers who previously shied away from the relative crudity of Ducatis? Or will it merely be a new status symbol for the colour-coordinated poseur?"

My feelings entirely, Mike, but then again we are both traditional Ducati enthusiasts of long standing and maybe the Paso will draw new customers to the marque. For this reason I am giving it a very much middle-of-the-road 3-star rating.

Indiana 1986-

If the Paso is a model to which it is difficult to give a suitable star rating then the Indiana custom bike is almost impossible. In its semi-chopper style guise it is just about as far removed from the traditional raw-boned Ducati sportster as any machinery on two wheels could be!

Ducati (read Cagiva!) obviously considered there was a need and market for such a bike. Originally Cagiva intended to offer one of the old bevel-driven 900 motors in an American-conceived custom bike, but this was eventually dropped in favour of the Indiana — first in 350/650 engine sizes, followed by a 750 in 1987.

Interviewed by *Cycle World* in their September 1985 issue, Cagiva boss Gianfranco

The Paso's cockpit.

Castiglioni said in reply to the question, will the American rider see a custom-style, Ducati-engined Cagiva soon? "Ah, this is supposed to be a secret, but we've already had a chopper-style bike made in California as a design study. So obviously the answer is yes, Cagiva wants to build a custom for the US." What the Cagiva chief did not reveal at the time was that the machine's début was a mere two months away, at the Milan Show that November.

When the Indiana appeared it sported all the usual custom goodies, such as teardrop gas tank, king-and-queen seat, pull back "bars", short, stubby mufflers, a fat 15-in. rear tyre, extended forks and, of course, masses of

The square-tube frame of the Paso — welding was not up to Ducati's usual high standard.

109

chrome plate.

No doubt the Indiana would sell in the States, and Italy too, but Ducati markets such as Britain and Australia, never! Somehow it was akin to producing a Porsche or Ferrari funny car.

Because of this its rating is a mere couple of stars.

Superbike 851 1988-

Ever since Ing. Fabio Taglioni had joined Ducati way back in 1954, the vast majority of the company's designs had flowed from the brain of this great man. During that time he had conceived a vast array of singles, twins and even fours for both road and track.

But one area he had all but ignored, except for a few racing prototypes, was four-valve cylinder heads. Instead Dr T. preferred to use the more simple two-valve layout, in both valve spring and Desmo form. At the end of 1982 Taglioni retired, at least officially, although he was still on hand in a consultancy role. The man chosen to succeed him was Ing. Massimo Bordi, who as already related

was a major figure in the development of the fully enclosed Paso. But Bordi's real début as a designer was with the machine which was the star of the 1987 Milan Show, the 851 Superbike.

This was an apt name for such an important model in the company's history. Not only was this Bordi's first design but it also broke new ground in many other ways. For a start it was the first production roadster to be offered with electronic fuel injection *and* ignition controlled by a pre-programmable computerized engine management system. Although a similar type had been available for some time on high-performance road cars, and had been widely used in Formula 1 car racing, Ducati were the first to employ it in the two-wheel world. For once the Japanese were not first . . .

Bordi was ably assisted by ex-racer and long-time Ducati man Franco Farne, plus engineer Luigi Mengoli and the rest of the development team. The prototype of what was ultimately to emerge as the 851 Superbike first appeared at the 1986 Bol 'dOr endurance race, albeit in 750 form. At the French circuit it

The 750 Indiana: the new owners, Cagiva, saw this model of particular importance on the Italian and American markets.

110

surprised racegoers and rival teams alike with its speed *and* reliability, staying together for over 15 hours. As the engine had only been completed a few days before this was some achievement. But it was to be some 14 months before the public was able to view the production version, now with a capacity of 851 cc (92×64 mm), and another six months before production got under way in May 1988. Two versions were offered – the "standard" model which retailed in Britain for £10,995 and the essentially racing model called the "kit" for £12,500.

A mainstay of the eight-valve Desmo V-twin was the Weber-Marelli fuel injection system. Ducati chose to use this for three main reasons: in their opinion the "open loop"-type was superior to the Bosch "gate"-system. The Weber had been derived directly from the type first used by Ferrari in their Formula 1 racing cars, and lastly Weber was based locally in Bologna, so ensuring that if any problems appeared they could more easily be resolved than with a company many hundreds of miles away.

And without doubt it was the 851's computerized fuel injection and ignition system which played such an important part and made it such a successful combination of the timeless virtues of the 90-degree V-twin layout and the up-to-the-minute technology of the late 1980s. With its water-cooling, two sets of double overhead cams and four valves per cylinder it was unlike any Ducati before it.

And to date most have agreed. However, things may not be as perfect as everyone has assumed. Sure, Lucchinelli had put in some excellent performances out on the track, but the *standard* models do not seem anywhere as quick, even though the "kit" version has been electronically timed at over 160 mph by *Performance Bikes* – in contrast the American *Cycle World* achieved only 154 mph, whilst the standard Strada should be good for approaching 150 mph. Speeds like this put the new Duke right up there with the fastest Japanese machinery.

But a voice of disquiet has come from self-

V-twin custom – the semi-chopper Indiana, available in 350, 650 and 750 versions.

111

confessed Ducati nut Alan Cathcart, who seems to be having second thoughts. In *Motorcycle International* dated December 1987, Alan's test of an 851 was headlined "8-valve Duke Italy's Future." Alan was so enthusiastic after riding Lucchinelli's racer that he promptly ordered a production 851 kit model for himself.

But by the July 1988 issue of the same magazine he was not quite so sure, and the headline read: "Is Ducati's answer to the RC30 Superbike all we'd hoped for? Yes and no." This time around Alan displayed a less than happy picture. For a start he was not happy with the performance, saying: "In its present form, I have to be completely honest and say that the 851 S (kit) is going to need a lot of work on the part of its customers to make it competitive in the Battle of the Twins racing, let alone in Superbike events against the cream of Japanese four-cylinder repli-racers like the RC30."

Cathcart also questioned: "Why only 851 cc, when regulations allow 1,000 cc for Superbike and BoTT racing?" He concluded by saying of the 851 kit: "It may look like a million dollars, but the reality is somewhat disappointing." Contrast this with some of the other test headlines, typified by *Motor Cycle News'* "stunner".

So who's right? Probably Alan Cathcart, after having paid out his own money, was disappointed that his customer bike was not in the same league as Marco Lucchinelli's factory mount. On the other hand, to give Alan credit, he did say that he thought the 851 would make an excellent fast road tool – and even went on to say he wished he could exchange his kit version for a Strada . . .

Only time will be the decider. In any case, as the 851, at least at present, is purely "limited production", this and its high price will mean that there are unlikely to be lots of secondhand examples floating around just yet. But on looks and engineering alone I have awarded it four stars.

750 Sport 1988-

With far, far less publicity from the world's motorcycling press than either the Paso or 851,

Introduced in 1988, the 851 Superbike set new design standards for the Bologna marque.

112

yet another Ducati V-twin appeared on the scene in early summer 1988.

This borrowed its name from the past, and 750 Sport to many meant the "old" bevel-driven Duke of the early 1970s – but in 1988 it also meant a new belt-driven "budget" (well at least by modern Ducati standards) sportster. Basically the new 750 Sport was a Paso engine in an updated F1 chassis and equipped with bodywork not dissimilar to the 851 Superbike. Powering the bike was a Paso-type engine, tuned to give an estimated 80 bhp. Like the Paso, the Sport used the reversed rear cylinder head so it could employ a twin-choke Weber carburettor. Tuning was restricted to upping the compression ratio and fitting higher-lift cams. A very visible round-tube frame carried 41.7 mm Marzocchi forks, and an alloy rear swinging arm with single shock, adjustable

for both spring preload and damping. A pair of cast alloy 16-in. wheels were shod with either Pirelli or Michelin radial tyres. Included in the specification was a Paso exhaust system, full fairing and a plastic seat hump which was removable to expose the pillion portion.

For very little development cost, the factory had succeeded in producing a distinctly sporting bike, and one which could well prove the most important in terms of pure sales figures by Ducati for many years.

Summary

I've included the current Ducati range to add extra depth to the book, but have only brushed lightly over them, as really they shouldn't be in a Buyer's Guide, which is largely intended as a guide to *used* rather than new motorcycles.

Chapter 16

Cagiva– How and Why

Cagiva is one of the very few success stories in the modern motorcycle industry – it is also an extremely complicated one – a phoenix which has risen from many fires.

Born in September 1978, it is currently the fifth largest motorcycle manufacturing group in the world and the largest outside Japan (if one discounts the communist bloc).

Currently this grouping comprises not only Cagiva itself, but Ducati, Husqvarna and Moto Morini, all three famous names which have been swallowed up in swift succession by Cagiva, in true David and Goliath style.

But before investigating how these amazing takeovers came about, it is neccessary to go as far back as 1912. This was the year when Aeronautica Macchi was founded for the manufacture of seaplanes. These early flying machines were built on the very site now used by Cagiva. Located on the outskirts of Varese, at Schiranna, the factory, with its slipways into the lake and its massive hangar, is located in an idyllic setting. What more could one ask for? – the tranquil waters of Lake Varese and in the distance the breathtaking and beautiful Swiss Alps. During the first World War Macchi built French Nieuport fighters under licence for the Italian army as well as flying boats of original design.

After the Armistice the company began a series of racing and record-breaking flying boats and seaplanes, including a succession of Schneider Trophy racers. It also captured the world aircraft speed record in 1934 at 440 mph.

Then came the Second World War, and the Varese company turned out what were generally acknowledged as the finest fighters used by the *Regia Aeronautica* (Italian Air Force). Soon after the hostilities ended, and barred from aircraft manufacture, Aermacchi decided to start peacetime production with a three-wheel truck. This proved a success (and is still being built by another company today). Then, anticipating the motorcycle boom and intending to have a stake in it, the Aermacchi chiefs looked for a good designer who would come up trumps. Their choice was Lino Tonti, who had been at Benelli and had worked on aircraft engines during the war.

Tonti's first design, a 125 cc two-stroke, made its début in 1950. It was both a commercial and sporting success – successfully competing in the ISDT (International Six Day Trial), which incidentally was staged around Varese in 1951. Tonti's final designs for Aermacchi, before joining rival FB Mondial in 1956, were a brace of cigar-shaped record-breakers.

He was replaced by Alfredo Bianchi, previously with Alfa Romeo and Parilla. Bianchi's first design for his new employers was the Chimera, a 175 cc push-rod single, with horizontal cylinder, but although expensively styled and widely publicized, it proved a poor seller.

Luckily for the company all was not lost,

114

Link with the past – the prototype 294 cc HD Cagiva was built in September 1978. Based on the old Aermacchi flat single, it never entered production.

In Britain actress Vicky Michelle was employed to publicise the new Cagiva marque.

however, and a simple un-dress exercise to produce a more orthodox motorcycle solved the problem. The result was to be a famous line of sporting roadsters and road racers, which are today held in such high regard by classic enthusiasts around the world. Less well remembered was the moto-cross version, which for several years dominated the Italian dirt bike championships.

And it was the success of these flat singles which played an important part in the evolution process. The American company Harley-Davidson were looking for someone in Europe with whom they could join forces to supplement their range of large-capacity V-twins. HD also wanted quality – and Aermacchi with their aviation interests (now revived) and their range of flat-single four-strokes appeared the perfect partners. This led the Americans to embark on a 50/50 commercial agreement with the Varese factory in 1960. With a lightweight boom developing in the USA they saw the push-rod singles in their road, racing and moto-cross versions as the ideal product.

Soon, lightweight Aermacchis fitted with HD badges were flowing into the US. For over a decade things went well, even though the infamous AMF corporate empire had taken over Harley in 1968. But the real problems started in

115

1972, when AMF bought out the remaining 50 per cent share in the Italian plant. By then Aermacchi had lost interest in two wheels and just wanted to get out of two wheels altogether.

Even though a record 45,000 bikes left the Varese production lines for North America in 1974 the writing was on the wall. With a combination of AMF's marketing tactics and Japanese competition, the sales of lightweight Harleys crashed Stateside.

Things were little better elsewhere. Outside the States, AMF had set up HD International, with headquarters in Geneva, Switzerland. This was simply a set of offices for the sales operation – the motorcycles themselves were built in Varese, and excess stock stored in Holland.

In practice HD International caused more problems than it solved. For one thing parts distribution can best be described in the mid-1970s as abysmal, there was poor quality control and a serious problem of over-production, so that by 1977 there were often two-year-old bikes in storage at the Dutch depot.

AMF had also set up an office in London during 1974 to market the range of Harleys in Britain, from the diminutive X90 mini-bike to the massive Electroglide V-twin. After selling in excess of 3,000 motorcycles in the British Isles, AMF closed their London Office in mid-1977.

It was at this point that I made the first moves to become the British importer for the Varese-built HD lightweights. Having been one of the original dealers appointed by AMF in May 1974, I had first-hand knowledge of the situation and felt that with impovements in quality control (which had already taken place), fresh stock (none of the "old" models from the Dutch warehouse!) and a proper spares back-up, the range of 125, 175, 250 and the new 350 single-cylinder two-stroke road and trial bikes would stand a much better chance of success. There were also 3,000 owners out there needing a source of spare parts. As someone who had acted as national parts distributor for various marques, including Ducati, Moto Guzzi and Derbi, I felt capable of doing the job correctly.

But it was January 1978 before the new operation, Mick Walker (Harley-Davidson) Ltd, began trading with a stock of motorcycles

1979 HD Cagiva SST 125. Although an old design, was the top selling machine in its class on the home market that year.

116

and parts, the latter *proving* that the Varese factory could supply the parts if they were ordered and from Day 1 we had almost 100 per cent availability! Initially sales went well, and we also received a good press for making a big effort on the parts front. In fact, everything was going well until the bombshell hit, news via a press story that AMF were pulling the plug on the Varese factory and there were to be no more HD lightweights! This must be taken in the context that we had only five months earlier signed a five-year agreement with AMF, making a considerable financial investment in building, staff, parts and motorcycle stock.

With so much investment we had no option but to continue and hope for the best, which in reality meant that the future looked bleak for the Varese operation, as AMF confirmed, when pressed, that their Italian arm was to be closed at the end of July 1978.

My controlling company Mick Walker (Holdings) Ltd was among the interested parties in taking over from AMF, but eventually the lakeside factory went back to Italian hands under the control of president Battisto Lozio and brothers Claudio and Gianfranco Castiglioni. The new firm, Cagiva, had taken over all the production rights for the range of ten road and off-road machines with single-cylinder motors, ranging from 125 to 350 cc. For an interim period (one year), the petrol tanks were to carry the name "HD Cagiva". But, gradually, the Harley name would vanish forever.

The Cagiva name was an amalgam of CA for CAstiglioni, GI for GIovanni, the father of the two brothers, and VA for VArese, and their company emblem an Italianized version of Harley-Davidson's Number 1 logo. Another feature of the Cagiva emblem was an elephant. Originally this was *white*, until I explained the significance this would have in English-speaking countries, and from that day on it became a grey elephant!

The Castiglioni brothers were successful businessmen from Varese who had seen their original company, formed by their father,

Cagiva's first off-road racer, the 1979 MXR 250 moto-crosser – based on a Harley design.

117

become one of the region's largest employers. They had made their fortune making locks, belt buckles, clasps and all those dinky bits of metal work one finds on luggage and handbags. The Castiglioni metal pressing operation was so efficient that it could actually beat the foreign competition on both price and quality.

When interviewed shortly after they had taken over the former AMF HD factory in 1978, Gianfranco, the eldest of the two brothers, was reported to have said in reply to a question, as to why had they bought the plant: "Because we love motorcycles of course!"

Indeed the Cagiva name was to be seen on the modified Suzuki RG500s of Franco Bonera and Marco Lucchinelli that the brothers sponsored *before* they became motorcycle manufacturers in their own right. And this enthusiasm for the sport was to remain a feature of the Cagiva operation, notably the millions which have been spent in a quest (so far largely unsuccessfully) for honours in the 500 cc road racing world championships.

Less publicized but far more rewarding has been their involvement with off-road sport, including trials, enduro and moto-cross. It is the latter where the real results have come.

One of the very first projects begun by Cagiva after September 1978 was the development of a water-cooled 125 cc moto-crosser. The prototype appeared in 1979, and went on

sale in the following May – the Japanese didn't have their water-cooled dirt racers ready until 1981 . . .

An enduro version, albeit air-cooled, was the next "new" Cagiva in the spring of 1981. Although they had no real experience of modern two-stroke dirt bikes, the Cagiva 125 moto-cross and enduro machines matched anything in the world, being fast *and* reliable.

Then at the 1981 Milan Show a whole host of new models appeared – a completely new six-speed 125 trail bike with up-to-the-minute styling, a water-cooled 125 enduro, an enlarged 200 version of the moto-crosser, the WMX250, a 500 moto-crosser and the company's first new four-stroke design, the 350 Ala Rossa, a single-cylinder ohc trail bike. Earlier in 1981 a brand new 500 cc two-stroke four-cylinder road racer had been débuted at the West German Grand Prix.

One may ask how all this was possible? One answer was money – lots of it. The other, people. When Cagiva commenced production a mere 130 workers had been retained from the original 500 HD staff. But of these over a *quarter* were in the R & D department. Not only this, but the Castiglionis spared no effort in recruiting the right people. Included were several technicians formally employed by the MV Agusta race team, top Dutch two-stroke engineer and tuner Jan Thiel and of

The successful British Army ISDT squad in 1981: numbers 282 and 243 are Cagiva-mounted.

118

course the former HD staff who had built and tuned the machines which had brought Walter Villa four world road racing titles for Harley-Davidson in the mid-1970s.

One must realize that when Cagiva entered the two-wheel world as a manufacturer, it had no new designs and no image, and outsiders gave it no chance of success in a highly competitive market.

But although the Castiglionis loved motorcycles, they still *thought* like successful businessmen. By emphasizing the fundamentals, efficient manufacturing, high quality, competitive pricing (by Italian standards), and authorizing new models, the fledgling company was able to achieve the seemingly impossible task of growing from nothing to be a world power within a decade, something no one except the Japanese have managed in recent times.

But all this would have been an impossibility without a buoyant home market. Here Cagiva was fortunate; at the time of their launch there was no competition from the Japanese – as they were barred from the Italian market in the classes which Cagiva

were concentrating on – up to 350 cc (although Honda and Yamaha have since built factories in Italy).

There was also the advantage of the considerable profit margin generated by selling the old designs and spare parts stock they had inherited from the previous owners over the first few months, and beyond. And a revised Harley, the SST 125, proved a best-seller on the domestic market during 1979-82. Another reason for Cagiva's success was that they were not too proud to examine in detail all the latest Japanese hardware. Inspecting the products of Nippon before setting down to design their own machinery meant that they were fully aware of the competition.

In 1980 Cagiva built 13,000 bikes and by 1982 this figure was up to 40,000. And there were now 300 workers, of which 50 were R & D staff. 1981 had seen the opening of the first foreign plant, when a factory in Venezuela began producing Cagivas for South America from parts made in Italy. This was followed by several other overseas projects, and as early as 1981 talks had taken place with the Soviet government into the possibility of supplying

Paris Show 1981: Bart Smith's 125 cc Cagiva world speed record breaker.

Cagiva expertise to the USSR in the same way as Fiat had done earlier in the four-wheel market. But to date the only concrete results of Italian-Russian co-operation came in 1982, when Russian riders rode the new 500 moto-cross bike in the world championship series – but don't rule out a tie-up in the future.

Ever since they had taken over the old Aermacchi/Harley-Davidson plant in September 1978 the brothers had dreamed even grander dreams. They envisaged Cagiva as the Italian choice, the company whose dealers would be able to present a complete alternative to the Japanese marques. But designing larger multi-cylinder four-strokes would take years and cost a fortune. So, instead, the Castiglionis scoured Europe searching for a partnership that could broaden the range more speedily.

During 1982 the Italian company took a detailed look at the British Hesketh factory, which went into liquidation that summer. But they backed out of this deal when sales director Luigi Giacometti discovered during a visit to Hesketh's Daventry factory that outside suppliers provided most of the components used in the V1000 V-twins' construction. Giacometti commented: "They (Hesketh) had nothing to offer us. The Receiver wanted £150,000 for a pile of drawings and papers."

Amazingly they found the answer to their prayers in their own backyard with Ducati, the legendary state-owned company whose reputation had consistently exceeded its profitability. On 2 June, 1983, Cagiva and Ducati executives called a joint press conference. Held in Milan this announced that Ducati would supply Cagiva with engines – for the latter company's new range of larger-capacity motorcycles (from 350 to 1,000 cc), and it was said to run over seven years. The Ducati name was to remain on the engines, but the bikes were to be marketed and sold by Cagiva. Funnily enough, it had been Ducati, owned by the state-controlled VM Group, which had made the initial move, quickly taken up by Cagiva. Ducati's problem was lack of demand, with large areas of factory floor space and plant standing idle, while Cagiva's was the opposite.

With this background one would have thought the June 1983 agreement made for a harmonious relationship. In practice just the reverse was true. The main stumbling block was Ducati's refusal to quit building their own bikes, and this really upset their partners in Varese. For almost two years there was an uneasy peace, Cagiva bought batches of engines, Ducati continued building bikes. Quite simply, at least from Cagiva's point of

Works rider Virginio Ferrari in action during 1982 on the Cagiva 500 GP racer.

120

view, the agreement was not really working out in a totally satisfactory manner, so to protect their long-term future the Castiglioni brothers, in early 1983, decided to acquire Ducati completely, and very quickly reached an agreement with VM to do so. On 1 May, 1985, the control of Ducati, lock, stock and barrel, passed from the Italian state to the private hands of Cagiva, and a new era was born.

Initially the brothers planned to retain the Ducati name for a short period only, as they had done with HD Cagiva, but soon realized that "Ducati" was worth just too much hard currency to drop – so except for a small grey elephant the Ducati name lives on and my guess is will do so for many years to come.

The brothers now had a comprehensive range from 125 to 1,000 cc, but felt they still needed one thing, style. Again a bold step was made. Massimo Tamburini, co-founder of Bimota and its chief designer for over 10 years, was recruited to the Cagiva team and charged with the job of creating individual exciting designs. Tamburini's skill was soon to be displayed with a whole succession of models, including the Ducati Paso and Cagiva Freccia to name but two.

The next target was North America, but here Cagiva, and even Ducati, had a problem: lack of reputation and an efficient dealer network. In typically simple and effective style the brothers solved it in one by purchasing the Swedish Husqvarna concern in 1986. Actually this solved another problem too. By then Cagiva were having to build their off-road bikes at the former TGM moto-cross factoy at Parma. With "Husky", the Varese brothers had not only a respected and well-organised set-up across the Atlantic, but yet more strings to their bow. Then, in 1987, yet another famous and old-established marque was added to the ever lengthening list of "name" conquests, that of Moto Morini.

Again there was logic behind the move. Both Ducati and Morini were in Bologna. The Ducati factory at Borgo Panigale had excess space, whereas the Morini factory at Via Bergami was in need of modernization. Morini had a new water-cooled V-twin with belt drive to single overhead camshafts and four valve heads at an advanced stage of development. And whereas the latest generation of Ducati's with eight valves were intended as 750s or larger, the new Morini engine was envisaged as anything from 250 to 500 cc.

Another development in 1987 was the opening of Cagiva Comerciale, a massive warehousing complex which brought the parts operation for all four makes under Cagiva control into a single unit, based next door to the Ducati factory in Bologna.

The 50th Milan Show, staged at the end of November 1987, saw the combined Cagiva, Ducati, Husqvarna and Morini stand as the largest and most impressive of the whole exhibition.

And so Cagiva marches on. The promise is there for a truly powerful European force in the motorcycle industry, something which ultimately can *really* challenge the Japanese, who have dominated the market since the early 1960s.

In 1978 there were no headlines, in 1981 one magazine's headline read: "Cagiva who?" Then in 1985 the American *Cycle World* said: "Cagiva: Today Italy, tomorrow the world." All this sums up the tremendous progress made by the Castiglioni brothers, who in a decade have achieved what many would have thought impossible.

But, what of the future, will this growth be continued, or even maintained in a world where powered two-wheels appear to be fading fast? The next few years will be crucial. If the Cagiva Group do get it right and finally establish themselves outside Italy, I would expect the ultimate dream to become a reality, that of all the machines being produced in their various factories displaying the uniform Cagiva logo and that name being accepted as *the* European motorcycle.

Only time will tell . . .

Chapter 17

Two-Stroke Dirt Bikes

★ ★	**Moto-cross models**
★ ★ ★	**Enduro models**
★ ★ ★	**Trials models**

History

Some might say that Cagiva owe their off-road sporting success to an idea inherited from the ill-fated AMF Harley-Davidson era.

It's true that Harley played around with the idea of a moto-crosser from the time a prototype appeared publicly in 1975. It's also true that a production version, the MX250, was sold in some numbers, exclusively on the North American market, during 1977 and 1978. But except for the original 250s, all the Cagiva dirt bikes were really their own work, and owed nothing to the factory's former management. Right from its earliest days Cagiva amazed the pundits by producing a succession of reliable, competitive and exciting dirt bikes in all major branches of off-road sport, moto-cross, enduro and trials.

Unlike their well-published and largely unsuccessful 500 cc World Championship road racing venture, which has cost the company millions and given very little in return, their dirt bike involvement has not only seen winning performances but a healthy and profitable return upon the investment made.

Moto-cross: MXR 250 1979-81

Alongside the *very* limited production and highly specialized RR 250 road racer, Cagiva's first attempt at building a competition bike was the MXR 250. This moto-crosser was clear-ly based around the bones of the earlier 250 Harley. Even so, Cagiva's engineers managed to convert it into a reasonably competitive and reliable bike for experienced clubmen, in the era directly prior to a major leap in moto-cross technology by the Japanese in this class.

The Harley-based 248 cc (72×61 mm) engine unit displayed its age by featuring simple piston port induction, flash chrome bore for its massively finned alloy cylinder, a five-speed gearbox and, or course, air-cooling.

Ignition was electronic by the Spanish Motoplat concern, and the engine sucked its mixture of petrol through a 38 mm Dell'Orto carburettor.

Compared to its roadster brothers, the engine was considerably beefed up for its task and featured straight-cut primary gears, modified clutch, strengthened big-end, forged, high compression Borgo two-ring piston and ported barrel amongst other changes. The power unit was housed in a strong double cradle chrome-moly tube frame, with the swinging arm in the same material, plastic tank, guards and side panels, 38 mm leading axle Marzocchi long-travel moto-cross forks, and Corté Coss rear units.

The MXR remained largely unchanged throughout its 3-year life except for the substitution of an alloy tank and swinging arm, and new design of air filter in 1980, and a German single-ring Mahle piston for its final 1981 season.

WMX 125 1980

Notable, as the world's first water-cooled production moto-crosser, the WMX 125 first appeared in prototype form in 1979, entering production in April the following year. There is doubt that at that time it was the most competitive dirt racer in its class anywhere in the world, but equally it was the least known. And this was why it failed to achieve the real success it should have gained throughout the summer of 1980.

When this bike was tested it was immediately apparent just what a superb machine it really was, causing a sensation everywhere it went. During the final two months of the 1980 racing season (September and October) we simply could not get enough bikes to meet the totally unexpected demand.

The WMX 125 owed absolutely nothing to anything which Cagiva had inherited when it had bought the factory, for it was all their own work.

Its single cylinder 124.63 cc (56 × 50.6 mm) motor, which was both air- *and* water-cooled, made use of magnesium for the outer engine covers, featured reed valve induction, a six-

The MXR 250 engine – the RX 250 enduro was almost identical.

speed gearbox, a 34 mm Dell'Orto carburettor and produced over 30 bhp, an outstanding figure for the time. The water-cooled alloy cylinder had a nickisel bore, which was much more robust than the cheaper chrome plate system. Ignition was a Japanese Nippon denso electronic unit. The frame again used chrome-moly tubing, but in a smaller gauge than on the air-cooled 250.

Up front there were 35 mm Marzocchi leading axle forks (with magnesium sliders)

Cagiva's first moto-crosser, the 1979 MXR 250, based on the old Harley design.

The 1980 RX 250, virtually an MXR moto-crosser, but with lights, centre-stand, tail pipe-cum-muffler and Sachs Hydragas rear shocks. It was a gold medal winner in the ISDT.

and at the rear twin Corté Cosso shocks with separate gas containers. Brakes had smaller 125 mm diameter discs front and rear (140 mm on larger bikes) and the super lightweight aluminium radiator sat above the front mudguard at the front of the fork tubes and steering head. This was another Japanese-made component, illustrating a vital facet of Cagiva company policy, that a part got on the machine only through quality rather than the country of manufacture. On the WMX 125 this

In 1980 Cagiva introduced the world's first production 125 moto-cross bike. The WMX used both air and water-cooling for the head and barrel.

showed up through items from not only Italy, but the USA, Japan and Germany. Its only really serious failing was a 428 size rear chain, which simply was not strong enough to cope with those 30 plus horses, and chain breakage was a common occurrence.

WMX 125 1981
The first batch of 1981 models retained the finned cylinder and head which gave the unique air- and water-cooling, but most 1981 WMX 125s featured a "bald" finless top end like the rival Japanese products. Other major differences consisted of a magnesium body for the 34 mm Dell'Orto, stronger 38 mm forks, longer swinging arm, new Corté Cosso "piggy back" rear shocks, wider 520 chain, single-ring Mahle piston, modified exhaust and several more minor improvements. There was also a change from red to silver for the tank and fork sliders and the alloy rims and rear sprocket were now finished in silver rather than gold. Overall it was a larger, taller bike, but stronger than the original. Although superior in its specification, it did not maintain the level of

124

advantage enjoyed the previous season.

A guide to just how popular the WMX 125 became in a short period was that some 350 were imported into Britain between August 1980 and October 1981, which, for a moto-cross bike, is some achievement. But the 1981 model was the victim of gearbox problems; as the importer we had to strip and replace gears on almost every bike and most before they were even sold.

WMX 125 1982

This was the year Cagiva stood still on the dirt racing front, at least at production level, and a year is a lifetime in the rapid development world of off-road racing. The WMX 125/82 was quite simply the previous year's model, but with a *heavier* steel swinging arm and a different colour, red, for the plastic-ware. It was also a year in which the factory learned the lesson, through poor sales, that moto-cross buyers are fashion conscious and 1982 was the year the Japanese first offered single-shock rear suspension to the off-road buyer across the board. Cagiva were left out in the

1981 saw the arrival of the RX 125 enduro with six speeds and reed valve engine. It was closely related to WMX, but air-cooled.

For 1981 the WMX dispensed with the head and barrel finning and relied entirely on water-cooling.

For 1982 the RX 125 became the WRX and became available in not only 125 cc, but also 190 cc engine capacities. Water-cooling meant it could run faster for a longer period than the original.

cold . . . but at least their gearbox was now bullet-proof.

WMX 125 1983

The big news for Cagiva fans that year was that the Varese factory had finally seen the error of their ways (I had pointed this out to sales director Luigi Giacometti back in 1981, and had been told that Cagiva knew all about single shock but *never* intended to use it!). The Japanese had as usual cleverly marketed a system devised years before but never really taken up. The Lords of Nippon had bestowed evocative names such as "Full floater" (Suzuki), "Pro-Link" (Honda) and "Uni-Trak" (Kawasaki). By comparison Cagiva's "Soft Damp" was somewhat lacking in charisma, but even so the Italian system worked supremely well and this together with other vital improvements and a restyling exercise brought back the buyers.

The engine received additional tuning, resulting in around an additional 3 bhp, and a larger 36 mm carburettor was fitted. There were also improvements in items which had proved prone to failure on the previous model. But besides the new rear suspension the biggest change was to the machine's style. In addition to the all-new plastic (red), the radiator was moved down behind the front down tubes of the frame and in front of the engine. Like its Japanese rivals there were plastic side protectors to guard against

The DG 350, a trials iron manufactured in co-operation with the Spanish Merlin company.

Its engine was based on the SST/SX 350 roadster unit.

126

damage. And yet again the exhaust system, including the tail pipe, was up-dated. All this added up to a completely new style which was a definite marketing aid, showing that Cagiva was fast learning that sales relied on not only mechanical excellence but an exciting and up-to-date appearance.

By 1983 the factory had begun to take a serious interest in the 125 World Moto-cross Championship and throughout the next two years the factory's 125 moto-crossers were painstakingly developed in the white hot cauldron of the Grand Prix circuit. This directly benefitted the production versions in the following season.

In 1985 Cagiva won the 125 world title for the first time, and in the process scored a major publicity coup.

WMX 125 1986

Named "World Champion Replica", the 1986 production model was truly a replica, and not just a cheap way of exploiting the factory's success the previous year.

The engine saw the biggest changes. Although it still retained the 56×50.6 mm bore and stroke measurements, virtually everything else was new. For a start the clutch and water pump swapped sides with the ignition; there were twin radiators for extra cooling; the head and barrel castings were square rather than round, but the biggest technical innovation was the introduction of an exhaust valve, described by the factory as CTS (Cagiva Torque Increase System). Power output (at the *rear* wheel) was a claimed 36 bhp. And the changes were not confined to the motor, for, in line with the dictates of a fashion-hungry buying public, there was a disc brake up front and new crisp styling to match anything coming out of Japan, all-in-all a bike which could compete with anything on the track. Few changes were made for 1987.

WMX 125 1988

The March 1988 issue of *Dirt Bike Rider* magazine carried the following headline to their test of the ⅛th-litre Cagiva moto-crosser: "WMX 125 – proven championship winner." Not only was this in response to more Cagiva world championship success, another title in 1986 and second in 1987, but the fact that by

now moto-cross enthusiasts around the world realized that Cagiva were no flash-in-the-pan.

DBR went on to extol its virtues: "The fastest riders among you will be delighted not only with the amount of power available (a claimed 37.5 bhp at 11,500 rpm) but also with the characteristics. Thought and technique reap rich reward. The power in this free-revving engine comes in sharply at the top of the mid-range. Shifting must be quick with fingers guarding the clutch at all times. The clutch itself is light and copes impressively with constant use or abuse.

The bike feels light and manoeuvrable, and this feeling inspires confidence in the rider. With this confidence comes speed. The White Power suspension at either end ably soaks up the worst in track conditions. You'll have to believe us when we say that this 125, in the right hands, will bring successes."

Dirt Bike Rider concluded "that only the price of £2,599 would hinder sales – but even so, you get a lot of bike."

WMX 190 1983-85

Although both the bore and stroke were different at 67×54 mm, the 190.38 cc engine was essentially an enlarged version of the smaller unit, even using the same 36 mm carburettor as the WMX 125/83.

1983 was the year in which Cagiva introduced its monoshock frame and the larger WMX was only built with this type of chassis.

In place of the 125's drum, the 190 sported a disc front brake, but except for an extra 3 kg (7 lb) the WMX 190 and the 125 were the same motorcycle.

However, even though it possessed a superior power-to-weight ratio, the larger machine could not recoup the 60 cc it gave away to the full 250s from the other factories and therefore was destined never to enjoy the success of its eighth-litre brother.

WMX 250 1988

For the first time, in 1988, Cagiva came up with a full 250 production moto-crosser. No, not a limited edition factory copy of the type campaigned by the factory over the previous couple of seasons but a ready-to-ride production racer available to the general public. And it created quite an impact even though, like the

125, it had a cocktail of parts from around the world. There was White Power suspension from Holland, Spanish Motoplat ignition, a Mahle piston from Germany, Excel rims from Japan and quality Italian brands such as Brembo, Fresco, Dell'Orto and Acerbis.

This time, unlike the old 190, the full 250 – 249.3 cc (70 × 64.8 mm) – was not simply a larger-capacity engine slotted into the 125 chassis. The wheelbase was longer and there was a full 10 kg/m (23 lb) weight difference and even the fuel tank capacity was different. Not only was there more power (a claimed 49 bhp at 8,000 rpm) but at 4.8 kg/m at 7,250 rpm, maximum torque was *double* that of the 125. The British price in 1988 was £200 more than the 125, at £2,799.

Dirt Bike Rider found all-in-all the new WMX 250 to be: "Quite a comprehensive package of quality parts. And this total package is capable of taking the right rider to the top of the class."

Perhaps this was to be expected when you looked at its pedigree. Internationally over the previous couple of years the works 250 had proved a real force. In 1987 Pekka Vehkonen came close to taking the World 250 Crown,

while 1986 had seen Jem Whatley take his bike to fourth in the title chase. This experience and the lessons learned had been put to good use in the production version.

MX 500 1983-84

The prototype of the 500 Cagiva Moto-crosser first appeared at the Milan Show in November 1981. However, it was to be well over a year later before the first production models were available to the public. This came after a none too good début on the Grand Prix circuit with a team of Soviet riders in 1982. Although much had been expected, in the final analysis this 481.9 cc (87 × 82 mm) delivered very little. Unlike the other Cagiva moto-crossers of its generation it was air-cooled and had a five-speed gearbox. Running on a 12:1 compression ratio, the massive "stroker" breathed through a 38 mm Dell'Orto carburettor. In its two-year production life it never sold in any numbers and was notably unsuccessful compared to its smaller brothers. It would probably have been dropped anyway, but the takeover of the Swedish Husqvarna concern in 1985 finally sealed its fate. The British price

For 1983 Cagiva finally bowed to fashion and brought out the WMX 125 in a monoshock form.

A 190 cc version soon followed and this was sold as the WMX 250.

128

in 1983 was £1,699.

Summary

At all levels, except in the 500 category, Cagiva have been highly successful in the world of moto-cross, with their machines gaining championships at club, national and international levels.

Even though the company have spent millions on their largely ineffective 500 cc road racing world championship venture, the Varese factory have gained much of their sporting fame from off-road sport, moto-cross in particular.

Star rating: Two firm stars

Even though their machines are truly world class, old moto-crossers make a very poor investment, however good they were in a particular year.

Some of the Cagiva dirt racers, such as the 1980 WMX 125, are worth saving purely because they were the first of a new breed. But generally speaking even a year-old bike has lost most of its new value. Not only is competition and development fierce, but the life expectancy, both in racing and mechanical terms, is extremely short. For example, today, even leading club riders usually need two machines in a season.

Perhaps the only real potential is to convert one of the moto-crossers into an enduro bike. Right from the early days the company realized this and therefore several models lend themselves to this new lease of life. Cagiva even offer a factory-produced enduro kit for some models.

Enduro: RX 250 1980-82

The RX250 was the bike which Harley never got around to actually making, even though it appeared in their 1978 catalogue. Cagiva

Replica of a World Championship winner: the 1986 production WMX 125 moto-cross.

129

realized the concept had potential and with a limited amount of development offered it for the 1980 season. The RX 250 was essentially an MXR moto-crosser, but with lighting equipment, chain guard, centre stand, fork gaiters, new exhaust system, new rear mudguard and Sachs Hydro-Cross rear shocks. A speedometer kit was also available as an extra.

Like the 1980 MXR, the RX had an alloy tank, making it completely street legal in virtually every country.

The RX 250, by winning a string of medals in many enduro events, including the ISDE (International Six Day Enduro), proved itself not only competitive, but a tough and reliable machine.

The final batch made in 1982 were renamed the Rally, but cosmetically and mechanically they were identical to the 1981 RX 250.

RX 125 1981
Clearly based on the successful WMX125 moto-crosser, the RX 125 was, however, air-cooled, and used the 1980 WMX as a base, rather than the 1981 model. Other changes included a steel swinging arm, a flywheel-mounted Motoplat generator, full lighting equipment, centre-stand and new rear mudguard and exhaust system. There was also an extremely neat and useful tank-top-mounted map case.

Which Bike? in their July 1981 issue, saw it as the "Smooth Option." This was a reference to the engine's power characteristics. *WB* commented: "The reed valve makes for a smooth power delivery and, as 125s go, the Cagiva isn't too peaky. Sure, the power comes in quickly, but it isn't all or nothing; it's much more tractable than the Fantic for example." They concluded by saying: "At £1,399 it's not a cheap 125, but in our opinion its worth the money – tractability and ride-ability count for a lot in enduros."

And, like the 250, the RX 125 displayed its ability, doing well even at international level, with a very respectable score of medals.

WRX 125 1982-84
First appearing as a prototype at the Milan Show, the WRX was, as the prefix suggests, water-cooled. Not only this but it inherited the improvements introduced on the 1981 model moto-crosser, such as stronger forks and the finless head and cylinder barrel. Unlike the moto-cross version, the WRX 125 retained the twin-shock frame until the very end.

WRX 190 1983-84
Marketed as the WRX 250, it was, like the moto-cross version, in reality a 190 cc. Few were made and by this time much of the interest shown by the factory in this branch of the sport had waned.

Summary
Except for 1980 and 1981, Cagiva never put as much effort into its enduro bikes as it did for the moto-crossers. Even so, they were fine machines and on a par with anything other manufacturers could offer. Compared with other similar Italian bikes they had the advantage of an "in-house" engine unit, broader spread of power, increased level of reliability *and* a higher level of build quality and finish.

Star rating: Three stars
An enduro bike is not in quite the same "throwaway" category as a moto-crosser, and because of this gains an additional star rating. Cagiva enduro bikes can be ridden on or off-road – unlike most serious racing mounts they came with fully street legal equipment, and their wider than normal spread of power makes them more pleasant to ride than many other enduro mounts, which have a far more fiery temperament.

Trials: DG 350 1982-85
The first Cagiva trials bike appeared as early as 1979. However, it wasn't until three years later that the company had a production version ready for the public to buy and then it wasn't really a Cagiva at all!

Known as the DG 350, this was really a product of Italian and Spanish co-operation. Since the mid-1960s Spain had led the world in trials bike development, but by the early 1980s its three leading marques, Bultaco, Montesa and Ossa, had all hit financial trouble.

From this chaos Ignacio Bulto, son of the Bultaco founder and the last remaining member of the famous family on the company's payroll, quit to go it alone. With a part-

130

ner, Juan Rigas, his intention was to form a new company which would concentrate its efforts solely on trials bikes, called Merlin, but as it would not have been financially sensible for the new partnership to design and build its own engine, they chose to buy an existing engine from Cagiva. So whilst Bulto and Rigas were responsible for building the chassis, the engine for the new trials iron would be a modified SX 350 roadster unit.

A prototype was built during the winter of 1981-82, and the manufacture of the first 200 machines began in April 1982. In Spain it was sold as a Merlin, and in Italy and certain other export markets, including Britain, as a Cagiva. And so the DG 350 was born.

The success of this venture ensured Merlin's survival and after 1985 they sold the machine exclusively as a Merlin. By this time the company had added a 125 cc version, which again was Cagiva-powered, with an engine based on the air-cooled, six-speed SXT 125/82.

Summary
Short and sweet, the combination of a Cagiva engine and Spanish running gear produced an overnight success. Today, Cagiva is involved purely in the supply of engine assemblies, to Gas Gas who took over Merlin during 1988 and remains one of the very few motorcycle producers (at least under Spanish control) left in Spain.

Star rating: Three stars
The DG 350, at least as a Cagiva, was short-lived, but nonetheless a competent feet-up mud plugger. Although never likely to command real classic status, it's still a rare bike, which may well be worth something in the future – hence its three-star rating.

Chapter 18

Two-stroke Street Bikes

★ ★ ★	**Aletta Oro 1985-87**
★ ★ ★ ★	**Freccia 1987-**
★ ★	**Other water-cooled models**
★	**Air-cooled models**
۱	**SST/SX 350**

History

For the first three years (autumn 1978-autumn 1981), the fledgling Cagiva concern continued to produce a basically unchanged roadster line-up inherited from AMF Harley-Davidson. This comprised eight piston-port single-cylinder air-cooled two-strokes of 125, 175, 250 and 350 cc, in both street and trail guise.

Cagiva were fortunate. Just before AMF had closed the old HD plant down, the company had up-dated its models with several worthwhile improvements – and added a pair of 350s.

This ensured that the new owners were able to offer a comprehensive, ready made, model range – without the usual expensive development costs. It also meant that the stock of parts and equipment already in the factory were fully utilized for maximum profit.

This profit was then ploughed back into the development of new all-Cagiva designs, first in the off-road field and then, from the 1982 model year, production roadsters and trail bikes for the mass market.

Harley-Davidson-based models 1978-86

The most successful of all these models for Cagiva was the SST 125. HD had created the SST a few months before it had shut up shop, and it was destined to become a best-seller on the Italian home market during the early 1980s.

The pedigree of the SST 125 could be traced all the way back to the ML 125 of 1967. By the early 1970s it had been given a flash chrome bore for its alloy cylinder, five speeds, an oil pump, and 12-volt electrics and was by then listed as the TX 125. 1974 saw it renamed SX 125 and a year later a major up-date saw it offered as the SS 125 (roadster) and SXT 125 (trail).

The SST 125 replaced the SS in 1978 and featured a whole host of improvements, including a disc front brake, electronic tacho, all-new instrument console and protected ignition switch (early versions had suffered from the ingress of winter). The list continued with new Ceriani front fork, new headlight, handlebar, a more comprehensive air filter and an improved kickstart lever. The trail SXT version benefitted from all the same improvements – except the disc brake.

With very little change the period 1979-82 saw the SST become Italy's top-selling 125, outselling all the rival manufacturers products. From 1980 it featured cast alloy wheels and electronic ignition was adopted for the 1982 model year.

Although the SST 125 survived until the end of 1984, a model based upon it, in customized form, known as the SST 125 Low Rider was still listed as late as 1986. This had all the looks to satisfy a budding Marlon Brando. *Motor Cycle News*, said: "The styling – though by no means everyone's cup of tea – is a far more successful interpretation of the Harley

The SS 175 roadster . . .

theme than the Jap factories' rather lifeless attempts." There were masses of chrome and polished alloy, high-and-wide bars, a two-stage seat, and sissy bar, complete with leather pouch and even a genuine HD V-twin rear light!

On the other hand the SXT 125 trail bike was replaced at the beginning of 1982 by an all-new Cagiva trail bike with its engine based on the successful RX 125 enduro unit. Confusingly Cagiva still labelled this completely new bike "SXT 125", which did nothing to help the poor parts man or customer . . .

The 175 had been introduced by Harley back in 1974. Compared to the quite ancient 125 engine, it had an oil pump, five speeds, and chromed alloy cylinder bore right from the start – plus the advantage of electronic ignition. That first year it was only offered in SX (trail) form. Half-way through the year it was joined by a 250 version – identical except for its larger capacity.

For 1975, SS (roadster) versions were added in both engine sizes. The following year the SS 250 became the SST 250 with the addition of a Brembo hydraulically operated disc front brake.

When Cagiva took over, except for some very minor revisions the SS 175, SX 175/250 and SST 250 continued. At the end of 1979 the 175s were discontinued and for 1980 the SST250 was up-dated, in line with the 350, with improved switchgear and electrics, a black (in place of chrome) exhaust system, higher bars, stronger wheel hubs and wider chain sprockets (a 530 in place of 520 chain size). A centre-stand and fork gaiters

. . . and SX 175 trail bikes were little more than Harleys dating back to the mid-1970s with Cagiva tank decals.

133

The SX 350, another model inherited from the AMF Harley-Davidson deal. Both the SST and SX 350s suffered from barrel and piston problems which were never fully resolved.

The SST 250/80. It was much improved over earlier models in several important areas, including switches, forks, brakes, chain/sprockets, seat and beefed-up engine.

completed the specification.

1981 saw a revised SX 250. This now had the wider chain/sprockets, and improved wheel hubs. An SX 350 exhaust system, two-part, with separate tail pipe, tucked in behind the left-hand side panel. The original SX 175/250 had no left-hand panel and the exhaust system was a one-piece affair with only a detachable baffle. Unlike the SST there were no fork gaiters, but a plastic front guard, rear mudflap and chrome lifting handle. Like the latest SST 250 the cylinder head and barrel were finished in black. Centre-stands were now standard on all the roadster and trail models. There were new colour schemes, including white and light blue (the latter with a matching blue dual-seat). The SST version now had cast alloy wheels and a stepped dual-seat.

1982 saw more improvements. The SST 250, now known as the Ala Verde (Green Wing), had a chrome exhaust, bikini fairing, rear carrier, modified clutch (with external operating arm) and several more minor changes. The SX

Cagiva's big sales success on the street during 1979-82 was the SST 125. Although based on an old Harley design dating back to 1967, it was the top seller on the home market in the all important 125 cc class.

250 became the Ala Blu (Blue Wing). This had mechanical changes from the 250 roadster, but also a revised exhaust system (still two-piece, high-level), a disc front brake, square headlamp with enduro-style plastic cowl,

The 125 Low Rider based on the SST: this was a custom bike which owed its styling to the Harley V-twins. All Low Riders imported into Britain came with wire wheels, not the cast type as illustrated.

The first of Cagiva's own designs for the street: the 1982 SXT 125. This six-speed trail bike owed much to the factory's dirt racers.

moto-cross-type plastic side panels, a new plastic rear mudguard to match the front assembly in the same material and a rear carrier.

With the introduction of the Ala Rossa 350 four-stroke trial bike in mid-1983 the 250 two-stroke was retained only in roadster form for the 1984 season. And it changed only in very minor detail until it was finally deleted from the model range in 1986.

The 350 two-stroke had been the final model designed by Harley-Davidson and very few had actually been produced before AMF decided to close the operation down in the summer of 1978. Whilst the pre-production prototypes had shown an excellent turn of speed (over 90 mph) and torque, the produc-

In 1983 Cagiva brought out the water-cooled Aletta Rossa. Although based around the 1982 SXT, it had, besides liquid-cooling, a front disc brake and monoshock and rising rate rear suspension.

tion models were a distinct disappointment. They vibrated, were prone to seizure (something the other smaller HD based two-strokes wouldn't do until they had run out of oil) and were no faster than the 250s.

In 1979 Cagiva's warranty claim department was kept busy replacing barrels and pistons from the 350s. It did not matter if they were SST or SX – both had the same weakness. In an attempt to cure the problem the pistons were modified with oil grooves and the barrels given a new type of coating. This partly cured the problem, but even then the vibration and insufficent performance continued. Generally the 350 strokers are not a bike I would recommend.

From 1980 onwards, the 350 models were up-dated in line with the 250s, the final model being produced in 1984.

What to look for
For a start, stay well clear of the 350. The others are reasonably reliable performers *provided* that you realize that they are technically very inferior to the later, Cagiva-conceived machines. Also unless owned by an enthusiast who is prepared to lavish tender loving care (which usually didn't happen very often) all the former HD models will deteriorate rapidly. The engines are generally reliable *provided* that the oil level is maintained. Like any mechanical thing they object to running on fresh air! On all models the oil tanks are hidden out of sight (the tank on the 175/250/350 is in the top frame tube!). The electrics on the three larger models can be a nightmare if they have been interfered with by someone who doesn't understand how they work. And as replacement parts like the CDI unit and the stator plate tend to be expensive my advice is whatever else make sure the electrics are working first before buying. By contrast the 125 (at least those with points ignition) are usually not only simple, but reliable too.

By the time Cagiva started making the HD-based models most of the real bugs (except the 350!) had been ironed out. They can never be described as exciting, but these early Cagivas handle well and are simple (except for the aforementioned electrics) to work on.

1978-79 SST 125s and 250s employed round

The final versions of the old air-cooled Harley-based 250/350 trail bikes were called Ala Blu (*Blue wing*). Although completely restyled they still used outdated mechanics.

piston pad calipers. These, unless lubricated regularly, tend to seize – often calling for a new caliper assembly. All disc-brake models from 1980 employed the much better conventional square pad-type and did not suffer this problem.

Finally, in a recent article for *Motorcycle Enthusiast* magazine I included the HD/Cagiva two-strokes in the *Practical Classic* series. Why? The answer I gave was as follows: "What is a practical classic you may rightly ask? Well, you can hardly hang this tag on a mega-priced Manx Norton or AJS 7R, nor for that matter something like a Vincent Black Shadow or even a BSA Gold Star. In my definition at least, practical means something that can be picked up at a reasonable, even cheap, price. It also means something which the average home mechanic can cope with. And perhaps most important of all, certainly if you are going to ride it regularly, a bike for which spares are still available."

As I also said: "Strange as it may seem, the Harley-Davidson (Cagiva) lightweight two-strokes meet all these guidelines."

In the mid-1980s the Elefant replaced the Aletta Rossa. It was available in both 125 cc and 190 cc engine sizes.

137

The larger Elefant, which came with the option of electric starting, was known as the E2.

Star rating: SX/SST 350 a megre half star, all other models one star

These star ratings are in line with the former Harley-Davidson models' lacklustre specification and performance. Also, at least at the moment, they can be picked up cheaply and are relatively plentiful (at least in Britain).

For 1985 Cagiva introduced the Kawasaki GPZ-styled Aletta Oro, a 125 cc super sportster with every extra from six-speed water-cooled 25 bhp engine to triple disc brakes.

However, the best of the bunch, the SST 125 and SX 175/250, are probably worth another star. They are just beginning to appreciate in value.

Air-cooled models 1982-87

The first of these, the SXT 125/82, made its début in late November 1981, at the Milan Show. It was Cagiva's first entry into the road market and as such is important in the company's history. It bore no relationship to the earlier Harley-based model with the same prefix.

At its heart was a detuned version of the six-speed reed valve unit used so successfully on the company's dirt bikes.

Its 124.63 cc (50 × 50.6 mm) engine was identical to both the water-cooled WMX moto-cross and the air-cooled RX 125 enduro models which had done so well in their respective sports.

The SXT 125/82 was air-cooled, and unlike the competition bikes used an oil pump rather than petroil mix. In its styling it was every bit as modern as the latest Japanese trail bikes and represented the first clear signs that Cagiva

138

would in future be a serious threat out on the street, just as much as it had already proved on the dirt.

Although the 1982 SXT was very much a "stepping stone" product – witnessed by the arrival of its water-cooled monoshock replacement, the 1983 Aletta Rossa – the engine was not completely scrapped.

Instead it was used to power the Aletta Electra 125. This was a new street bike to replace the by now ageing, but still popular, SST 125 model in the all important home market. In appearance the newcomer *looked* like an SST, but with monoshock rear end and new-style cast alloy wheels. Like the final model of the long-running SST, the Aletta Electra, had as standard equipment, a small fairing, rear carrier and fork gaiters.

Other differences included a completely new silencer, side panels and most interestingly an electric start, hence the Electra tag.

Unlike the SXT 125/82, the Aletta Electra was never exported to Britain.

Besides being modern lightweight designs, there is little to excite the bigger bike enthusiast, both these models clearly being aimed at the beginner. The only parts which seem to give trouble in these machines are the piston, big-end and main bearings, especially if they are allowed to run short of oil. Otherwise both are remarkably troublefree, if unexciting.

Water-cooled models 1983
Like the six-speed air-cooled 1982 SXT 125, Cagiva chose to launch their foray into the water-cooled production roadster league with a trail bike, the Aletta Rossa. This was clearly based around the older bike, but with the added advantages of liquid cooling, monoshock rear suspension and several more minor improvements. When I tested an Aletta Rossa for *Motorcycle Enthusiast* in early 1984 its engine impressed me with its snappy and torquey performance (which I couldn't believe was restricted to the British 12 bhp limit), excellent handling on tarmac or dirt and its easy-to-live-with suspension, which was light years ahead of the previous model's twin-shock layout, Cagiva registered this as "Soft Damp" – which compared to the Japanese version didn't sound very good even though it per-

formed exceptionally well. The Aletta Rossa was also the first Cagiva mass-production model to feature the wide use of plastics; in fact there was virtually no chrome plate anywhere on the bike.

At the end of 1983 an up-market version appeared. This was the Elefant 125. Besides more power (in de-restricted form) it also featured a two-tone dual-seat, larger-capacity tank, alloy wheel rims, a 4.60×17 rear tyre (in place of the Aletta Rossa's 3.50×18), and a wider-section 3.00 (2.75) 21-in. front tyre. Fork gaiters, modified front mudguard with anti-spray front portion and stronger 35 mm front forks completed the picture.

Next, in 1984, came a larger-capacity model, the Elefant 200. This utilized the same 190.38 cc (67×54 mm) engine size of the early WXM 250 moto-crosser and pumped out around 30 bhp, giving a top speed of 87 mph (against 70 mph of the smaller version). Another change was an increase in carburettor size, up from 24 to 25 mm.

Dimensionally both machines were identical in 1986 and the Elefant 2 replaced the original. But except for revised cosmetics, a more comprehensive radiator shield and a tail pipe for the larger model, the "new" Elefant's were identical, but more expensive!

When testing the Aletta Rossa back in 1984 I had formed the opinion that the basic engine and frame would make an ideal basis for a

By 1987 the Aletta Oro was dated, such was the fierce competition in the Italian 125 stakes, so Cagiva launched the Massimo Tambarini-designed Freccia, its most exciting roadster ever, with GP styling and near 100 mph maximum speed.

superb lightweight sports roadster. Cagiva obviously thought so too, because in 1985 they introduced the exciting Aletta Oro 125. With 25 bhp at 9,000 rpm on tap, and the styling of a Kawasaki GPZ Superbike (even down to the firecracker red and black finish!), full fairing, cast alloy wheels and triple discs, the 90 mph flier with its electric start luxury could have expected to have sold thousands, but they didn't. Technically the bike was more than a match for its rivals at the time, but although sales went well initially, by the summer of 1986 Cagiva had been overtaken in the sales charts in the all-important 125 Italian category by not only Honda's Italian arm, but also rivals Aprilia, Gilera and even Laverda.

In response, Cagiva used the talents of former Bimota co-founder and chief designer, Massimo Tamburini, who had joined them in early 1985 and designed the running gear of the Ducati Paso, to create a new eighth-litre super sportster.

The result was one of the most stunning small-capacity motorcycles of all time, the 125 Freccia (Arrow), introduced in the spring of 1987. Alan Cathcart in his book *Dream Bikes* said: "The Freccia's visually striking styling would look good on any bike, but on a relatively humble and inexpensive 125 cc single it may well be the most motorcycle for the least money, in real terms, yet put on the market." Cagiva claimed a power output of 27 bhp at 10,000 rpm from the six-speed water-cooled unit. For the first time on one of their production bikes Cagiva used a gear-driven balancer shaft, which all but damped out any vibration which might well have been there on such a high-performance engine. There was also a GP-type exhaust valve developed from the factory's four-cylinder racer.

Maximum speed was a *genuine* 97 mph – achieved by a couple of independent sources with full electronically operated timing equipment.

Unlike the Ducati Paso, the tiny Cagiva's frame was a work of art, although manufactured in chrome-moly steel, it was painted silver and thus to the casual observer (once the bodywork was removed) looked like alloy. This was assisted by its high level of finish.

And unlike so many Italian motorcycles of

the past – big or small – the Freccia's technical merit didn't just hang on its engine, frame or suspension.

Smaller, often overlooked details were equally impressive. Things such as what looked like a fuel tank was actually a fold back cover under which were three separate tanks – for fuel, oil and water. The instruments and switchgear, for so long magazine testers' chief complaints on Italian bikes, for once matched or surpassed anything currently available to buyers of Japanese machines.

And as for the colour scheme, well, red wheels, red seat and a combination of red, white and yellow made for a bike which really grabbed attention – of Bimota proportion! Which, after all is not really surprising as the man who created so many dream bikes for the famous Rimini marque was responsible for the Freccia.

The only real criticism which could be levelled was the lack of a centre-stand.

What to look for
Very few water-cooled Cagivas (besides off-road bikes) have come to Britain, and in any case it's too early with models such as the Freccia to advise on long-term defects. I've included the latest models for much the same reason as in the Ducati section – because of interest, rather than that anyone will be restoring one just yet!

Star rating: Freccia four deserved stars, Aletta Oro three stars on technical merit, other water-cooled models two firm stars.

Summary
Although Cagiva have gained much publicity from their tie-up with Ducati, it is nonetheless a fact that the company's expansion has been achieved with the sales of small-capacity single-cylinder two-strokes. So don't scoff – just appreciate that nobody continues to buy bikes for long if they aren't good. To succeed in the highly competitive world of lightweight motorcycles you have to first build well-made, reliable, practical bikes which everyone can afford – and then do this year-in, year-out. Cagiva have managed this and richly deserve their success.

Chapter 19

Ala Rossa

★ ★	**Ala Rossa 350 1983-86**
★ ★ ★	**T4 350E/R 1987-**
★ ★ ★	**T4 500E 1987-**

History

Cagiva's first four-stroke, the Ala Rossa (Red Wing), made its public début at the Milan Show in November 1981. But it was to be almost two years before it finally entered production in the autumn of 1983. The reason behind this lengthy and intense development process was the company's realization of the importance that it had to get things right first time with such an important design.

This was summed up by Cagiva sales director Luigi Giacometti, shortly after the Ala Rossa had entered production: "It's our first four-stroke product and we have to be 101 per cent certain it won't give problems once the owners have them. I've calculated we've lost 3,000 sales to other people like Morini and so on who've produced a similar bike since ours was revealed, just because we wanted to get it right. We even took a couple to the Sahara to make sure they'll work well in the Mojave Desert and the Australian outback!"

One can fully understand the company's insistence on making sure the bike was as near perfect as possible before letting customers loose on it. Not only was it Cagiva's first thumper but at that time (late 1983) the Varese concern was only five years old and were fully aware of the fact that one wrong move could put their efforts back months, if not years.

It was also their first middleweight series production bike which did not have its roots

firmly buried in the outdated technology inherited from the factory's Harley-Davidson days. With the Ala Rossa, and the new two-strokes they have conceived during their short life, Cagiva could at last cock a snoop at those who had earlier regarded the company's products as nothing short of a joke, at least outside Italy.

The Ala Rossa was hardly earth shattering, but it clearly signalled the factory's bold, inventive attitude, which was to become a characteristic of Cagiva's drive to match the corresponding Japanese product in every way except cost. And therein lay something of a dichotomy. For in their attempt to manufacture a soft, neatly engineered four-stroke single with monoshock rear suspension they had produced a machine with a distinctly Japanese look *and* feel. Even so, the design was still the first all new Italian 350 cc single-cylinder four-stroke since the days of the bevel-driven ohc Ducatis and push-rod Aermacchis to reach mass production status.

All in all a brave, bold move.

350 Ala Rossa 1983-86

In many ways it was hardly surprising that Cagiva should have chosen to design their own four-stroke – given that several of the development team had been deeply involved in producing the successful range of push-rod singles back in the late 1960s and early 1970s under the Aermacchi HD banner. In fact,

The prototype 350 Ala Rossa as it appeared at the
1981 Milan Show: it was Cagiva's first four-stroke.

A pre-production Ala Rossa, photographed in the
summer of 1983.

when the Castiglioni brothers had taken over in September 1978 it had been planned to release a rehash of the old flat single. But this idea was soon shelved − as the plant's new owners felt, probably correctly, that they had to go forwards not backwards. This was not before at least two prototypes with an engine capacity of 294 cc had been built.

They realized that the world had changed a considerable amount since the last production 350s had rolled off the Varese line in the summer of 1974, and so had four-stroke motorcycle engine technology.

For one thing, the other three Japanese concerns, besides Honda, had joined the club. This had meant more competition and faster developments, leaving the rest of the motorcycling world struggling to keep up, let alone a company which had only just come on to the scene.

However, as events were to show, Cagiva was not a company to accept the status quo, or one which was interested only in a small, specialized niche of the two-wheel market, like, say, Ducati, Laverda or even BMW. And for continued expansion, not only did Cagiva

have to broaden their range but also take the export market seriously, which meant coming into conflict with the Japanese. The Ala Rossa was just such a machine to give them a chance. Like the Japanese, and unlike the niche manufacturers, it was not particularly bad at anything, nor was it strikingly good, it just worked.

The Cagiva-designed, chain-driven, sohc engine could have come out of any of the Japanese Big Four's product line, with its appearance, design and typical Oriental over-square dimensions of 82×65 mm, which added up to 343 cc. The alloy cylinder with its cast iron reborable liner and alloy head, were inclined forward 13 degrees. One of the few design features which proved it was not entirely of eastern concept was the caged roller bearing big-end. The two-valve engine was safe to 7,500 rpm while providing a very flat torque curve which operated from 4,000 to 7,000 rpm, with maximum torque figures of 2.55 kg/m at 6,000 rpm.

Like certain Yamahas, including the XT 550 model, the engine of the Ala Rossa was fitted with a system which automatically opened the

The Ala Rossa was finally launched in the autumn of 1983. The photograph shows the version sold from then until late 1985.

exhaust valve when the kickstarter was depressed slightly, dispensing with the need for a valve lifter, and giving easier starting. There was a distinct lack of mechanical noise, with the exception of the primary drive gears. The Dell'Orto PHF32 carburettor was effectively silenced by a large under-seat air filter keeping induction roar to an absolute minimum. The exhaust note was also well subdued – in direct contrast to the majority of Italian trail bikes.

The gearbox was five-speed, with a typically Japanese-style left side one-down, four-up operation, whilst a primary kickstarter meant it could be started in any gear.

A double-cradle tubular frame provided good handling and safe roadholding, helped by the combination of excellent Metzeler enduro-pattern tyres, a 27-degree steering head angle, 190 mm travel 38 mm Marzocchi front forks and a single Corté Cosso rear shock absorber, which provided 200 mm of travel.

The monoshock swinging arm was even given the "Soft Damp" logo in typical Japanese style. In fact, the rear suspension was perhaps the finest feature of the whole machine. The *Motor Cycle* tester commented: "Cagiva have

obviously learned much from their increasingly successful involvement in moto-cross and enduro machines and the Ala Rossa handles with a genuine quality."

A single hydraulically operated cast iron 260 mm diameter Brembo disc looked after the stopping power up front, whilst an equally effective 160 mm drum controlled the rear, proving more than enough to retard the progress of the 154 kg (dry) machine.

But it was the combination of a up-to-the-minute style and attention to detail which really set the Ala Rossa apart from other European trail bikes of the era. The various switches and instrumentation were the equal of any to be found on Japanese machinery, while the 12-volt, 150-watt, Kokusan-Denko flywheel generator and electronic ignition. After all this praise one could have been forgiven for thinking that here was a perfect combination. But there were a couple of snags, one of them performance – or lack of it.

The Ala Rossa's 25 bhp was barely 250 cc standard, let alone 350 cc. This, coupled to the machines undergearing, resulted in power characteristics which could be termed soft or just plain gutless, depending on your

The restyled Ala Rossa made its début at the Milan Show in November 1985.

144

honesty. Below 4,500 rpm, the motor felt much like any other middleweight four-stroke single, solid and torquey, but from then on, and certainly from 5,000 rpm upwards, it gave the impression of working hard and the level of vibration increased considerably. Such was the undergearing (at least for road use) that you needed 7,000 rpm, by which time the vibration was upleasant, affecting hands and feet in particular, despite rubber-mounted footrests.

A highest one-way maximum speed of 83.21 mph was recorded by *Motor Cycle* in their May 1983 test, with the tachometer needle diving into the red by 800 rpm! This was against the manufacturer's *claim* of 86 mph. *Motor Cycle* also averaged 61.3 mpg throughout the test. Even though performance and vibration were worse than many would have liked, in all other areas the Ala Rossa scored well, giving anyone who rode it the lasting impression of a solid and well-built motorcycle. Cagiva had also succeeded where other Italian bike builders, notably Benelli, had failed, to

In September 1986 the four-valve 350R T4 was launched at the Cologne Show in West Germany: it replaced the two-valve Ala Rossa on the production lines.

build a Japanese-type bike to Japanese-type standards.

In 1985, the Ala Rossa received a cosmetic up-date, but mechanically remained unchanged.

Then in 1987 came a total redesign, with the

Milan 1987 and the début of the 500E T4, a machine comparable to any half-litre single from Japan.

145

Ala Rossa being superseded by a trio of *almost* entirely new machines, including a larger-capacity version.

T4 350E/350R 1987-
Although retaining the basic engine used in the Ala Rossa, including the bore and stroke measurements, virtually everything on these newcomers was different from the model they replaced.

In the redesign the engine had been given four valves, twin exhaust ports and different carburettors, 350E: 32 mm Bing; 350R: Dell'Orto 34 mm and a balancing shaft, in an attempt to both increase power output and reduce vibration levels. This resulted in a substantially improved unit with power output and improved engine torque figures over the Ala Rossa. The E produced 33 bhp, the R 33.8 bhp, and they shared maximum torque figures of 3 kg/m at 7,000 rpm.

At 139 and 132 kg respectively, the 350E and 350R were also lighter and this was mainly achieved through the wider use of plastic, a square-section alloy swinging arm for the monoshock rear suspension, and lighter, smaller-diameter brakes: a 240 mm disc at the front and a 130 mm drum at the rear.

Instantly noticeable was the aggressive off-road styling. They looked like genuine enduro machines, even though they were mainly intended for on-road usage. Besides the new appearance their specification was also greatly different from the older model, with larger 40 mm Marzocchi front forks, high-tensile alloy wheel rims, a new frame with a single front downtube (the new swinging arm already mentioned) and even a large sump bash plate.

All-in-all a pair of impressive on-off roaders.

T4 500E 1987
But the really big news, although largely unreported in the foreign press, was the T4 500E, Cagiva's largest, non-competition, non-Ducati-engined bike to date.

The larger capacity was achieved by increasing the cylinder bore by 12 mm, giving the massively oversquare dimensions of 94×65 mm and a capacity of 452 cc. Running on a 9:1 compression ratio and with a 40 mm Bing carburettor, but otherwise much the same unit as the 350E/R models, the big single pumped

out 40 bhp at 7,000 rpm. Not only this, but the torque figures were improved by 25 per cent to 4 kg/m at the lower engine revolutions of 6,000 rpm.

Finally, with a dry weight claimed to be identical to the 350E, the larger machine appeared to offer a significant improvement in the performance stakes. But even with the advantages of a balancer shaft, it is liable to vibrate more than the smaller unit and to be less economical on fuel. Cagiva claimed a maximum speed of 96 mph, compared to 90 mph from the new 350s. The 500 was obviously aimed at the export market, while the 350s were for the home market.

What to look for
With all the models, except the Ala Rossa, only just appearing on the market this section is therefore difficult to compile. Because, quite simply, we don't know what is *really* good, or bad, where it really matters – in service. But, as has been proved with the Ala Rossa, the Cagiva four-stroke single line is generally solid and reliable. And it would appear that the factory has finally acted to eliminate the two major failings of their original design, power and vibration.

Star ratings: Ala Rossa 1983-86 two stars, T4 350E/R and T4 500E three stars
Even though all these machines have more Japanese influence than Italian, at least in their concept and execution, they are nonetheless one of only two truly home-grown Italian four-stroke singles in the middleweight class (the other is Gilera). Perhaps they are not classics in the true word, but they are efficient and modern motorcycles in their own right, and as such should be purchased for use rather than as any form of investment.

Summary
Like their own two-stroke designs, Cagiva have proved that they can create modern motorcycles to match anything coming out of Japan. This I feel has been the key to their success, particularly whilst the home market remained protected from foreign (Japanese!) imports. Now this is changing it will be interesting to see if Cagiva can truly compete . . .

Chapter 20

V-Twins

★ ★ ★	**Elefant 600/650/750 1984-**
★ ★	**Elefant 350 1985-**
★ ★	**Alazzura All Models 1984-86**
★ ★ ★	**Alazzura GT 1986**

As revealed in Chapter 16, Cagiva's original reason of wanting to be involved with Ducati was not complete motorcycles but engine units. This meant V-twin engines with a capacity of 350 cc and above.

Following the June 1983 press announcement that, in future, Cagiva and Ducati would be doing business – in other words Ducati would be supplying Cagiva with engine units – the Varese company went ahead at full speed to put on offer not only street bikes with the Taglioni-designed Pantah motor but, perhaps most noteworthy of all, an on-off road Paris-Dakar-styled V-twin dirt bike.

Continental Europe had made the Yamaha Tenere its best-selling larger-capacity motorcycle during the early part of the 1980s. This had resulted in machines with the radical styling of the Paris-Dakar marathon parked almost everywhere you looked.

The Castiglioni brothers, who owned Cagiva, realized the significance of this, resulting in the on-off road machine being given the highest priority. Called the Elefant, the prototype made its public appearance at the Milan Show in November 1983 amidst a fanfare of trumpets from the press corps.

Elefant 600 1984
"No-one would have believed it a few years ago – one of Taglioni's V-twin street racer motors powering a trail bike. Nothing less than pure sacrilege," so said a *Motor Cycle News*

road test of the production version of Cagiva's Elefant. But while Ducati purists may well gnash their teeth there was a very good reason for such a move: money! Desert-styled racers were big business in Italy. For example, in 1983 Italians had purchased more Yamaha Teneres than any other street bike larger than 350 cc.

But in Britain things were somewhat different. As *MCN* put it: "Paris-Dakar replicas raise about as much excitement in a Brit Biker's blood as a CZ 350 running on one."

Even so the 90-degree vee-twin had all the right credentials for being shoehorned into an off-road chassis: it was narrow, compact and relatively light. The icing on the cake was the power delivery, which, with its large amount of torque and wide power band were just right for the dirt too.

The first models that Cagiva offered had the 583 cc, (80×58 mm) engine, but by the end of 1984 the capacity had been increased to 649 cc, achieved by increasing the bore *and* stroke to 82×61.5 mm. At the same time the compression ratio was lowered from 10.4:1 to 10:1 and in addition the overall gear ratio was lowered to give brisker acceleration, but the larger cubes meant that the top speed of just over 100 mph was unaffected.

Elefant 650 1985-87
The Elefant received a considerable boost to its prestige when Herbert Auriol took his Legier-sponsored works-prepared model to seventh

147

position in the gruelling Paris-Dakar Rally in January 1985. The event won (for the last time) by BMW, proved the Cagiva over perhaps the toughest terrain a motorcycle could ever meet. In an event covering 7,500 miles and lasting 22 days, only just over 100 of the 550 competitors completed the course in which cars, trucks and motorcycles all competed. A year later the same rider looked certain to win the event before an accident near the end put him out of the running.

Obviously Auriol's machine wasn't entirely standard. The standard front forks simply wouldn't have been up to the job for real competition use. However, the rear suspension really worked, being at its best on bumpy back roads, where the Ohlins single shock combined with Cagiva's own rocker arm "Soft Damp" system amazed me during a test session in 1986; I just couldn't fault the rear end. In contrast, the 42 mm leading axle telescopic front forks just were not in the same league. Although they coped off-road, at least at the speeds I managed, on road, over ripples, they complained, particularly at higher speeds and over white lines, ruining high-speed handling.

The job of pulling the 400 lb Elefant down from speed was handled by single discs front and rear. And although there was enough power up front with the four-pot Brembo caliper, the heaviest braking again showed up

The first fruits of the Cagiva-Ducati link forged in June 1983 were the Alazzura V-twin, with a choice of 350 cc or 650 cc Pantah engines. The photograph shows the 650 version tested by the author during the summer of 1985 for *Motorcycle Enthusiast* magazine.

deficiencies in the forks, which started to squirm about. I considered that the combined extra length of the legs and the use of a plastic mudguard meant that some form of fork brace was required. With this fitted I am sure the 650 Elefant would handle with the best of them.

MCN had this to say about the engine: "Always the acceptable face of Italian motorcycle engines, the Pantah motor manages a rare blend of character and efficiency."

During my time with the Elefant, and even though the maximum output of 52 bhp could not be called stunning, it was nonetheless sufficient to never give an impression of being strained. With its smooth torquey delivery, you did not need to thrash through the five-speed gearbox searching for the power band. In fact the power flowed in from a low of 2,000 rpm, right up to the red line of 7,500 rpm, above which it simply ran out of steam. This sort of torque meant that "wheelies" could be pulled in almost any situation.

The American *Cycle World* magazine got a standing quarter-mile figure of 13.39 seconds and 97.16 mph, and broadly agreed with *MCN* by saying: "Cagiva has created a motorcycle with some stunning strengths and few substantial weaknesses."

The hydraulic clutch (like all later Pantahs) had become considerably lighter than the unit first fitted to the 600 SL Ducati back in 1981. Attention to detail was another area where it scored over some of its pure Ducati brothers and even the switchgear won praise from journalists! But, of course, like any two-wheeler, there were faults.

Perhaps the biggest was the seat. For a start any trip over 50 miles was a real pain – and to make matters worse still the seat height was a towering 36 inches! This made the Elefant one of the tallest trailsters around, even with a 17-in. rear wheel rim. It was also certain to attract attention, *MCN* commenting: "Buy an Elefant and you won't need the real thing (i.e. full-size *elephant*) to attract attention – the Cagiva has a high enough profile as it is."

Elefant 750 1987-
Called the Lucky Explorer, this replaced the 650 version during late 1987. The first most pressmen saw of it was on the company's stand at the Milan Show that November. In

many ways the 750 was a much more serious bike than the machine it replaced. Not only was the engine bigger and more powerful, but it was clearly based around the latest works Paris-Dakar desert racers. The 748 cc engine size had been gained by boring out the cylinders by 6 mm to 88 mm with the stroke remaining unchanged. Running on a 10:1 compression ratio the motor now gave 60.5 bhp at the higher engine speed of 8,000 rpm. Torque was a massive 6.3 kg/m at 6,000 rpm. The clutch was still hydraulic, but now dry rather than wet.

In place of the twin 36 mm Dell'Ortos were a pair of Bing 64/32/375 instruments. The original 12-volt 200-watt alternator had given way to a more powerful 300-watt assembly.

The appearance of the bike was considerably different from the earlier machines, with brand new plastic bodywork. This included a huge sump guard, and there was now a low-level front guard with a built-in fork brace. This was a direct answer to criticisms already made. The fork tube diameter remained unchanged.

Instrumentation displayed the care which Cagiva had given this area, including a speedometer (with odometer) which was far more accurate than is usual on an Italian motorcycle, matching tachometer, pilot lights, turn signals, idle and beam lights, battery recharge, and low oil pressure warning lights. In the appearance stakes it matched anything the Japanese had to offer and like its predecessor was a poseur's delight.

Suspension offered 210 mm of travel at the rear and 195 mm at the front, giving the rider a fair degree of comfort − provided of course he could put up with the tall seat height . . .

Cagiva claimed a maximum speed of 107 mph, but once again it was the engine's wide spread of power which was the most important consideration and advantage, both on and off road.

Elefant 350 1985-
Mainly intended for home market consumption where motorcycles of 350 cc and under are grouped in a far more advantageous tax bracket, the 350 Elefant was, like any other smaller Pantah, distinctly underpowered and far more revvy than its larger-capacity

The 650 Alazzura GT. Besides an increase in capacity, the model benefitted from improved rider protection and higher quality finish.

brothers. Not only was maximum power, at 33 bhp, considerably less, but so was engine torque, which had been reduced to 3.51 kg/m at 7,000 rpm (almost half that of the 750) and at the same time far higher up the rev scale.

Maybe the only thing going for it was the sturdy build. In size, it was identical to the larger-capacity machine and even the suspension, brakes and wheel rims were identical. Of course this did not assist performance, but Cagiva still claimed a maximum speed of 94 mph. But of course speed is only half the story for a dual-purpose bike . . .

What to look for
For a start very few Elefants − of any capacity − will have been ridden seriously off-road. In fact most will have been used more as a rich man's toy and therefore not only will they be little used, but will usually be in pristine condition. But expect a wide variation in prices, depending upon which country you reside in. This will depend on how popular the Paris-Dakar-style bike is in your particular location.

Mechanically at least, the engine assembly is virtually bullet-proof. By the time the Elefant entered production all the early bugs had long since been ironed out of the Pantah engine, which had entered production back in 1979. And Cagiva had made it a policy of not only using the best materials and components, but concentrating on a high level of excellence of their build quality. All in all, the Elefant is firmly recommended, *provided* you can live with the particular type and style of machine, which is best described as a Range Rover on two wheels: rugged, powerful and expensive.

Star rating: Elefant 600/650/750 three stars, 350 two stars
Very difficult, you either love or hate this type of motorcycle. I guess the former would award a few five stars, the latter a solitary one star. I've plumped for three, mainly because underneath its brash exterior it is a well-built, competent and reliable *trail* bike, with the breeding of a genuine desert racer.

Alazzura 600 1984, 650 1985-86
Like the Elefant, the Alazzura (Blue Wing) began life in 1984 as a 600 (read 583) and shared the same state of engine tune, but with higher overall gearing for its intended role of a touring/sports roadster. It received the larger 649 cc engine capacity in time for the 1985 season.

The Alazzura also came at a time when Cagiva were planning on building their own range of Ducati-powered bikes. This was before they finally acquired the whole Ducati set-up, lock, stock and barrel, in 1985.

Not only was the engine really a Ducati, but the chassis too – the Alazzura's frame coming straight off the same Verlicchi production line. So much of what has already been related in Chapter 13 applies here too.

But if the basics were the same as the

The Elefant, a Paris-Dakar-styled on-off roadster. Produced with a choice of 350 cc, 650 cc or 750 cc power, it has proved Cagiva's top selling four-stroke.

Bologna-built Pantah, lots of the balance definitely wasn't. The ride was less harsh due to the softer damping specified for the Marzocchi forks and the softer internal spring rate in the remote reservoir rear shocks. This gave the bike a civility missing from the pure Ducati original. The almost flat bars and slightly rearset controls contrived to produce a riding position which *Motor Cycle International* described as "Eminently suited to city work, touring and, if you hunker your shoulders down a little, back-road scratching too."

Although a clearly more civilized motorcycle, with a greater attention to detail than the original Ducatis, the Alazzura was not without its problems. For one thing it didn't have that magical name on the tank, and in some important areas Cagiva had not been too successful. The seating, whilst suiting someone over 6 ft, was of less comfort to someone, shall we say, of more modest build. And whilst a seat height of 31½ in. wasn't as mountainous as the Elefant, it isn't low either. Switchgear and instrumentation was the good side of acceptable, but the mirrors were simply awful. As *MCI* so rightfully said: "With their rubber shrouded elbows and massive plastic frames, they look like something rejected from the Italian version of *Star Wars*." Not only that but as I found out for myself they vibrated hopelessly over, 5,000 rpm.

The same publication concluded their road test of a 650 Alazzura in the August 1985 issue by saying: "Cagiva have rightly concluded that an Italian bike need not lose its unique *brio* if the rough edges, normally delivered with the package, are suddenly removed."

In my opinion though, by removing "the rough edges" Cagiva also succeeded in removing some of the charisma, character if you will, of the Ducati versions. Somehow the Alazzura just did not have it; maybe it was lack of style, maybe it was the civilization process, or maybe it was simply that I was riding a Cagiva rather than a Ducati . . . but whatever it just did not seem the same. As if to confirm this feeling Julian Ryder giving a second opinion to *MCI's* test said: "The Cagiva didn't do it to me, though (he was talking about character). It is definitely faster (claiming a maximum speed for the 650 of 125 mph) and better equipped than any other Pantah-engined bike, bar the

150

F1 replica of course, but the vibration annoyed me and the sit up and beg riding position just does not seem to go with the rest of the bike, certainly, not if you compare it to the exquisite 600 Ducati."

But a *third* opinion (Colin Schiller) did not agree: "I thought the bike (the Alazzura) was a gem. I'd rather have one of these than ten XBR 500s."

Reviewed in retrospect the Alazzura was a serious attempt to make the Pantah appeal to a wider audience. In doing this Cagiva created a machine with far less flair than the original, but far more practical: the straight touring handlebars, the softer suspension, even the addition of such items as a helmet lock and a clock told you this. For *everyday* use it was superior, but somehow it just didn't create the original sparkle.

Alazzura 350 1985-86
Simply the 650, but with the smaller engine. So it was underpowered and unexciting to ride, but cheaper on tax and insurance, and more economical on fuel.

Alazzura 650 GT 1987
The final variant, and also the best. For a start it stopped trying to play the combined roles of tourer/sportster. The GT tag really did mean *Grand Touring*.

The most obvious difference was the stylish full fairing, rather than the much smaller cockpit affair on the earlier models. But this was just the start, for there was a more comprehensive front mudguard, different cast alloy wheels (with six, instead of five spokes), a wider-section 120/80 H18 rear tyre, a dry clutch (still hydraulic) and an all-black engine unit and exhaust system. In place of the previous red and silver colour scheme for the bodywork was a more restrained metallic charcoal and white, with red lining. The whole effect was to give the machine a more complete and attractive look. Even so, like the other Alazzuras it could hardly be called a sales success and in any case by this time not only had Cagiva swallowed up Ducati but also realized that by using the Ducati logo potential customers were far more likely to shell out lire, pounds, dollars or yen. So thereafter Cagiva swallowed their pride and did good commer-

cial business by concentrating exclusively on Ducati at the Superbike end of the market (with the exception of the Elefant big-bore trail bikes). Meanwhile the Alazzura in all its versions was quietly pensioned off and deleted for the range of Cagiva and Ducati models, without the majority of the motorcycle world even blinking an eyelid.

The final model, the 650 GT, was sold in Britain for £3,495 (1987) – this was some £2,000 cheaper than the *cheapest* Ducati (except the Indiana custom bike) at that time.

What to look for
As an investment don't . . . even though the Alazzura is a practical roadster, the 650 GT in particular. Very few were imported into Britain, for without the Ducati name nobody was really interested. A few were converted into Formula 2 replicas for either street of track use (the basic bike was closely related to the 600/650 Pantah).

The Alazzura was also the first street bike which Cagiva offered in North America and leading tuner Reno Leoni even race-kitted one!

Reliability, as with all Pantah engines is good. In fact the whole design was fairly sound, but even so there were hardly queues lining up to buy an Alazzura when it was new and things haven't changed much now that its secondhand. The only advantage of this is that you can take your time in making up your mind and probably get one with a bargain basement price tag.

Star rating: Standard models two stars, 650 GT three stars
Only two stars are awarded for the standard model, not because there's anything wrong with the motorcycle, just that it's not a particularly popular bike – too middle of the road for the usual enthusiasts of Latin motorcycles, yet with not enough appeal to the buyer who would normally opt for a Japanese machine. Another factor which did not help matters at the time of its launch was not enough people knew who Cagiva were, at least outside its native land. For all these reasons the Alazzura was perhaps doomed right from the start. A pity really, as the final version, the 650 GT, is a damned fine middleweight tourer.

Chapter 21

Owners' Clubs

Today the marque owners' club is more popular than ever and Ducati owners world-wide have shown their interest in belonging to some sort of organization where they can meet other enthusiasts with like-minded interests. Although much more recent, Cagiva owners are now following the trend.

The first Ducati club, certainly in Europe, was proposed some 30 years ago, when *Motor Cycle* published details in their 16 April, 1959, issue. Londoner L. Gillbanks was the preliminary organizer, but as far as is known nothing became of this early attempt. However, with the help of British importer and enthusiast Vic Camp, a Ducati Owners' Club was successfully launched some six years later, with the club magazine being edited by Vic's wife, Rose. This enterprise seems to have survived for about three years before going out of favour.

It was not until much later, in 1975, that together with Stephen Finch of Kenilworth, Warwickshire, I was instrumental in getting a new DOC into being. This time the club has survived until the present time. Sadly Stephen was killed some years later in a traffic accident, but without his enthusiasm it is quite likely there would not have been a British DOC, or at least not until later. Strangely though a great lover of Italian bikes, he never actually owned a Ducati.

In 1985 there was a major re-shuffle of the whole club and its outlook, which has resulted in increased membership and a more outward-looking set of officials.

I should add, except for being an honorary member I have never played an executive role in the running of the club or become involved in its politics.

In the last decade the Ducati Owners' Club theme has spread world-wide and there are organizations catering for fellow enthusiasts on every continent.

The British DOC hold an annual gathering during TT week in the Isle of Man and also organize rallies and the like, and most European clubs hold rallies and race meetings. For example, the French DOC organize an international Ducati race meeting (as does the Dutch club) as well as Battle of the Twins race at Le Mans and a national series.

Likewise in the rest of the world. As you will notice from the useful names and addresses there is already a large list (and I've not included everyone) and it is growing.

Cagiva owners meanwhile now have their own organization thanks to Peter Bartlett of Leyton, London. This is known as the HD-Cagiva Two Stroke Owners' Club.

Back in 1980 one Richard Dicks from Cambridgeshire had got things off the ground in the way of a Cagiva Owners' Club, but this, like the original Ducati projects, was too early, and the club soon folded.

Clubs are very much a personal choice. I am not of the opinion that every Ducati of Cagiva

A non-standard 750 GT owned by Maggie Church, seen at the British DOC's National rally, 1984.

An immaculate 1979 900 SS owned by British DOC member Russ Cooke. Often a concours winner, he says, "It's my pride and joy, I live for the bike. I get as much pleasure out of cleaning it as riding it."

owner should join – some people just are not club types, preferring instead to go their own way, but in my experience are nonetheless enthusiastic because of it. So just because you do not belong to the DOC and COC does not matter, in the same way as just because you do not go to church does not mean you are not a Christian. With that example I've probably started a few people writing letters . . .

Useful addresses
Ducati Owners' Club Austria
Ewald Grillmayer
A M Rosenhügel 15
A-3500 Krems
Austria

Ducati Club Muchen
Ducati Club Deutschland
Wolfgang Gobel
Beethovenstr 16
D-8034 Germering
West Germany

BMF Rally, May 1988. Mick Tarrant's superb 250 racer was a highlight of a professionally organized display put on by the DOC.

Ducati Club Denmark
Peter Leisted
Hammerichseij 1B
3200 Helsinge
Denmark

Ducati Club Schorndorf
Lothar Fredenreich
Mulstr 23
7076 Pluderhausen
West Germany

Ducati Club Finland
Petri Makijarvi
Vvorimiehenkatu 14 A 16
0014 Helsinki
Finland

Ducati Club Hanover
Wolfgang Riess
Weidemannweg 8
D 3000 Hannover 91
West Germany

Ducati Club France
Section Nord
Lionel Regnat
9 Rue de la Croix
77720 Grand Puits
France

Motoclub Ducati ADM
Via Bentini
38-40128 Bologna
Italy

Ducati Club Sweden
Lars Ekeman
Sandviksvägen 5
16240 Vallingby
Sweden

Ducati Owner Club Switzerland
Marcel Aebi
Dorfstrasse 141
8424 Embrach 2H
Switzerland

Ducati Owners' Club of Victoria
PO Box 16
Box Hill
Victoria 3128
Australia

Ducati International Owners' Club
PO Box 650857
Miami
Florida 33265-0857
USA

Ducati Owners' Club GB
Alan Yardley
131 Desmond Drive
Old Catton
Norwich
Norfolk NR6 7JR
Great Britain

Ducati Owner Club Japan
1-4-30-101 Miyawaki-Cho
Takamatsu-Shi
Kagawa-Ken 760
Japan

HD-Cagiva Two Stroke Owners' Club
Peter Bartlett
Flat No 1
2 Hainault Road
Leyton E11 1EE
Great Britain

Chapter 22

Annotated Bibliography

Cathcart, Alan. *Ducati Motorcycles*, Osprey Publishing, 1984. 224 pages.

The first full history of the marque has been a best-seller around the world. Generally well researched and detailed. But text gets somewhat jumbled. Coverage of both production and racing machines from the 48 cc Cucciolo clip-on engine unit through to 1983 when the first moves came concerning the eventual takeover of the Bologna company by the Cagiva concern.

Cathcart displays his love of racing by providing some excellent photographs and detail to this side of his work.

Useful in general terms rather than as a source of information regarding an individual model, but still highly recommended.

Cathcart, Alan. *Ducati – The Untold Story*, Osprey Publishing, 1987. 128 pages. Essentially a collection of photographs, the majority in colour, of prototypes, racers and specials.

Hardly lives up to its title, as besides the picture captions, there are very few words indeed. Nonetheless the excellent standard of production and photography go some way to making up for this.

Once again racing takes pole position. If you are feeling down on a winter's evening, with motorcycling weather or any meets being months away, this book will help bring back the memories. But don't expect to use it as a source of reference.

Cycle World On Ducati 1962-80, Brookland Books, 1987. 80 pages.

Essentially a collection of road tests and articles reprinted from the respected American magazine *Cycle World*. Mainly covers the various singles, but also a preview of 750 GT, 860 GT test, 500 GTL (parallel twin) test, 900 Darmah SD test and concludes with an Owners' Survey of the bevel-driven V-twins.

Clymer, Ducati Service & Repair Handbook 160, 250, 350, 450 cc, through 1974. Clymer Publications, 1975. 130 pages.

A workship manual-type publication covering both narrow and wide-case ohc Ducati singles. Based upon the factory's own workshop manual (now no longer in print), although up-dated. Lots of useful information not only for a major stripdown but general servicing too.

Eke, Stephen. *Ducati Tuning*, Lodgemark Press, 1986. 112 pages.

Not quite what the title implies. This book concentrates upon the bevel-driven roadster V-twins and covers most aspects of their preparation for optimum on-road performance. Includes details of carburettor specs, actual jettings and vacuum gauge readings – plus useful fault-finding tips and an engine strip of an early 750 GT.

Haynes, Mark 3 and Desmo Singles Owners Workshop Manual, Haynes Publishing Group,

1979. 116 pages.

Another workshop manual, this should have been the best around, but unfortunately there are a number of errors. A sister manual deals with the early bevel-driven V-twins, up to the end of 1977, the 860 GT, GTS, early 900 GTS, early 900 SS and 750s.

Renstrom, Richard. *Great Motorcycle Legends*, Haessner Publishing Inc., 1977. 128 pages.

A revised version of the book by the same author entitled *The Great Motorcycles*, this contains a chapter dealing with Ducati's history until the early 1970s. Compared to Alan Cathcart's later book, this is really basic stuff.

Rivola, Luigi. *Racing Motorcycles*, Galley Press, 1977. 320 pages.

Although there are only a few pages in this book devoted to Ducati, the lovely colour illustrations make it worth getting for these alone. Four Dukes featured: 1958 125 Desmo single, 1960 250 Desmo twin, 1972 750 Imola and 1976 860 Bol d'Or.

Schiller, Colin. *Fast Bikes – The New Generation*, Osprey Publishing, 1987. 128 pages.

In amongst the very latest megabikes from the industrial empire of Nippon are details of the Ducati F1 and Paso – plus Bimota's Pantah-engined DB1. Buy this book for its colour photography rather than the written word.

Scott, Michael, and Cutts, John. *The World's Fastest Motor Cycles*, The Apple Press, 1986. 128 pages.

The authors chose to include not only the Ducati F1 and Mike Hailwood Replica Mille, but also Cagiva's 650 Alazzura. Like *Fast Bikes* there's also the Ducati-engined Bimota DB1. Nicely produced but lacking any real information.

Walker, Mick. *Ducati Singles*, Osprey Publishing, 1985. 192 pages.

This work established the author's literary reputation. Acknowledged as the "bible" by owners of the Bologna singles world-wide. Covers all known production models plus the various racers. Appendices contain specifications, colours, carburettor settings, prices, model recognition.

Walker, Mick. *Ducati Twins*, Osprey Publishing, 1985. 192 pages.

Companion volume to above.

Over the years there have also been numerous general news stories, technical articles and road tests of both Ducati and Cagiva. Obviously, for reasons of space, if nothing else, it is impractical to attempt a full listing here.

Chapter 23

Sources of Parts

Although it might appear easier to deal with your local friendly dealer, my advice is don't. For a start its unlikely that he will stock very much in the way of parts which will fit Ducatis and even if he has the odd oil filter or clutch cable for a Pantah, it's highly unlikely he will have anything for older models.

Another point, from personal experience, is that it takes a *minimum* of five years for someone to become knowledgeable enough in Ducatis to be able to do the job properly, however much that person may wish to please.

Knowing what fits where on a particular model takes time, so for once experience really does count for something.

To Ducati's credit, for many, many years, unlike concerns like Guzzi who have sold off spares for the various single-cylinder models, the Bologna factory maintained a stockholding of parts way back to the original ohc model of 1957 vintage. However, recently, as a partner in the family Ducati parts business (Rick & Mick Walker), I have noticed that the new owners Cagiva don't appear to be interested in *any* of the bevel-driven models, which does not bode well for the future. As demand is still there perhaps, hopefully, they will change this policy. Meanwhile it seems increasingly likely that the specialist parts dealers will have to take over the responsibility by remanu-facturing parts as they become unavailable from the factory. My company has already

begun this process by making available such items as virtually every decal, Desmo single rear-set items and pistons for 200 ohc models, in batches. As this process is expensive and time-consuming there will obviously be a limit to exactly what can be re-manufactured. Items such as cylinder head castings and crankshaft flywheels are a prime example, for they are simply too expensive and likely to sell in exceedingly small numbers.

Besides new items, there is the question of used parts. Provided these are serviceable they can often not only solve a problem if a new item is not available, but will also be cheaper (or should be!). Recently, with the price of complete machines rising rapidly, far fewer motorcycles have been broken for parts and this process is likely to continue, so making used parts more difficult to find.

Therefore on the surface both new and used spares would seem to be rather difficult to find. Happily, at least to date, this has not in practice proved the case. This is mainly due to certain specialist dealers being able to purchase stocks of spares from former Ducati agents who have closed their businesses. And so it is still possible to get a large percentage of what you need.

Long term, as these stocks dwindle, the position is far less certain. But as I write this in the summer of 1988 it is still possible to get most engine and cycle parts for a 1958 157 Sport – not bad for what after all is a 30-year-

What every Ducati enthusiast loves to see,
a warehouse full of parts for his favourite bike.

old motorcycle!

What bits can't you get? Well, larger cycle parts like tanks, seats, side panels and mudguards are most obviously in short or even non-supply. Traditionally, engine bits have been easier to find, but obviously each model has its own particular shortages.

My advice is if you normal supplier cannot come up with the part you need try someone else for he might just have that elusive item tucked away somewhere. Also remember the world is growing smaller through more efficent communications – try a foreign supplier if necessary.

Finally there are autojumbles, or even resort to advertising . . . but in any case don't give up.

British Sources: Ducati Parts
Spares GB, 1 Walpole Road, Colliers Wood, London SW19 2BZ. (All models.)

Moto Cinelli, 13 Midland Road, Olney, Bucks MK46 4BL. (V-twins after 1978.)

Newton Equipment, 281 High Road, Leytonstone, London E11 4HH. (Particularly customizing equipment.)

Witty Ducati, 107 Manor Road, Caddington, Nr Luton, Beds. LU1 4EF. (Particularly single-cylinder racing equipment.)

Rick & Mick Walker, 10 Barton Road, Wisbech, Cambs PE13 1LB. (All models.)

British Source: Cagiva Parts
Harston Motorcycle Centre, 104 High Street, Harston, Cambridge, CB2 5QB.

Chapter 24

Used Bike Market

Whatever the star rating and whatever your personal secret desires (two-wheeled of course!), there is one other very important factor: money . . .

Buying secondhand gives you much more flexibility in this area, or at least it should.

Before you even start you must have your finances fully sorted. This includes how much you are going to limit your spending to, and how you are going to borrow the money if you have not got the amount needed already in your bank account. With credit, obviously shop around for the very best deal.

Once this is settled you can start looking seriously. Where you look first is really governed by which country your live in and which model you have set your heart on.

The best buys, or in other words value for money, are usually the machines which do not even reach being advertised. But conversely these are the most difficult to find if you are looking for an exact model and will not be satisfied with anything else.

The annoying thing is for all you know just the bike you want may well be sitting in someone's lock-up garage hidden from view to the world, and with its owner wanting to sell, but not knowing how to go about it, or just too lazy to actually advertize it, just round the corner!

The following are the more accepted ways of finding a used bike:

1 Local newspaper – in the classified section.
2 Local dealer.
3 Specialist motorcycle press classifieds.
4 Specialist dealer.
5 For older machines – autojumbles and the like.

What you have to bear in mind is that a machine purchased privately will not normally be covered by any form of warranty, whereas one from a dealer will be subject to the various trading standards law of a particular country. Even so, with careful and intelligent work it *is* possible to make some excellent buys privately, and most Ducati/Cagiva owners are genuine enthusiasts themselves, so you are less likely to be offered a "rouge" without knowing it. But don't *assume* that everything is right; check it or take someone along who has the necessary technical ability.

There are obviously other ways of finding the right bike, through race meetings, club magazines, rallies and even other owners.

If all this fails why not try placing an ad yourself? Probably the best method is to use any of the specialist magazines that operate free classifieds to their readers. Normally these are the monthlies, so this will require waiting a few weeks. For "instant" results you will have to use something which appears weekly (*Motor Cycle News*, for example, in Britain), but then you will have to pay.

159

Many 250 Mach 1 models ended up as racers – either from new like this 1964 example being raced by Brian Jefferies the following year – or converted later.

Finally if you are purchasing an older machine which carries the classic tag, make sure your insurance cover is on an agreed value basis. Many insurance companies now operate a scheme where an older motorcycle can be covered in this way. It will certainly save you a lot of heartache, not to say anything of financial loss, if your pride and joy is later damaged or stolen.

To give British and American readers a guide, there follows a list of the specialist magazines which are the best bet to find a Ducati or Cagiva advertized, or to place a wanted advertisement yourself.

Useful names and addresses:

Great Britain
Motor Cycle News, PO Box 11, Huxloe Place, High Street, Kettering, Northants NN16 8SS.

Silver Machine, 32 Paul Street, London EC2A 4LB.

Classic Bike, EMAP National Publications, Bushfield House, Orton Centre, Peterborough PE2 OUW.

The Classic Motorcycle (as for Classic Bike).

Motorcycle Sport, Standard House, Bonhill Street, London EC2A 4DA.

Motor Cycle International (as for *Silver Machine*).

One to stay clear of – not a Bologna-built Ducati single at all, but a 24 Horas (Hours) produced by the Spanish Mototrans factory.

Classic Mechanics, Bob Berry Publishing Services, Suite G, Deene House, Market Square, Northants NN17 1PB.

Performance Bikes (as for Classic Bike).

USA
Cycle, 1 Park Avenue, New York, NY 10016.

Cycle World, 1499 Monrovia Avenue, Newport Beach, CA 92663.

Cycle Guide, PO Box 5120, Philadelphia, PA 19141.

Motorcyclist, PO Box 3296, Los Angeles, CA 90078.

Cycle News, PO Box 498, Long Beach, CA 90801-0498.

Motorcyclist's Post, PO Box 154, Rochdale, MA 01542.

Walneck's Classic 'Fieds, 8280 Janes Avenue, Woodridge, IL 60517.

A typical Ducati dealer's showroom.